Love Breaks Through

Love Breaks Through

Miracles of Love in Kenya

Katie MacKinnon

with
Lynda Neilands

Christian Focus Publications

© 1988 Katie McKinnon
First Christian Focus Publications Edition 1992

Reprinted 1995

ISBN 1 85792 027 9

Published by
Christian Focus Publications Ltd
Geanies House, Fearn, Ross-shire,
IV20 1TW, Scotland, Great Britain

Cover design
courtesy of
Centro de Literatura Crista

Printed and bound in Great Britain by
Cox & Wyman Ltd, Reading, Berkshire

CONTENTS

Grateful acknowledgement is made to
Hodder and Stoughton Ltd.,
for permission to quote from
Something More by Catherine Marshall © 1974
and to
Miss Dorothy Chalmers
for permission to quote extracts from her letters.

Thanks are also due to
Jean Chalmers,
and to
Elisabeth Struthers and Neville Frith
for their invaluable help and encouragement in the
preparation of this book.

Foreword

In February 1976 I heard for the first time about Katie MacKinnon and her babies. As secretary of the *Stichting Redt Een Kind* (Dutch for Save a Child Foundation) we had come into contact with the Africa Inland Church of Kenya, and we had started to send support for a children's home in Ogada. I received a letter from Rev C M Kinzer, one of A.I.M. missionaries in Kenya, and in this letter he said:

> I'm writing concerning another need here in Kenya. At Litein we have a small hospital and maternity work. We also have a children's work going on there in connection with the medical work. Miss Katie MacKinnon, the sister-in-charge, has been caring for small infants in her home for a number of years and this has given her many opportunities in the villages where the children come from for presenting the claims of Christ. The local people have been backing this work with their prayers and some of them have been giving her small amounts of money and food for the children. Katie has been doing this all from her own income. The work is growing and the other day I met with Katie along with church and local leaders to discuss the possibility of expanding this work.

There are now ten infants at Katie's home which
have lost their mothers at birth or are too sick to go
home. In a number of cases there just is not any
place to send the children once the mother is dead.

Imagine getting a letter about a nurse in Kenya who
from her own missionary allowance takes care of ten
babies in her own home.

We live in a time where egoism reigns supreme and
then one hears of a person who gives all she has: her time,
her energy, her love, and all her money, to take care of ten
little Kenyan babies. I was impressed. That must be
someone who loves the Lord very much and wants to use
her special talent to care for babies, in His service.

Later on that year I visited Kenya and I met Katie in
Litein. I had been looking forward to this meeting to see
what Katie did. It was not a disappointment; on the
contrary, it convinced me of her calling to rescue babies
from hunger, neglect, poverty and death. I found it a great
privilege that we could help her financially.

That first visit was also the beginning of our friend-
ship. Katie has been a tremendous help to me. The
number of A.I.C. children's homes that we support in
Kenya grew and Katie often accompanied me when I
visited these Homes, and also some in Uganda. She was
not only a good companion with an enormous sense of
humour, but she often drew my attention to things that
could be improved.

You can read in this book how Katie moved from
Litein, to Mulango and from there to Kitui. I visited her
there some months back for the last time. I was even more
impressed than before. It is a joy to see those little ones
playing and when they see you they immediately come

running to you. Especially when they see Katie. These are the toddlers; the babies, of course, are in their beds. There are always some children sick or very underfed. They get special attention. Katie and her helpers give them all the love and care which they need. There were sixty babies and toddlers the last time I was there.

In this book Katie tells about her life. She certainly does not minimize her shortcomings, but her dependence on the Lord is very obvious. I hope that many people will read this book and that they will realise what a wonderful work the Lord is doing in Kenya through Katie MacKinnon and her babies.

Anky Rookmaaker

CHAPTER ONE

AUNTIE SEONAID

Two o'clock! The minute hand on the kitchen clock was vertical at last.

'If we don't go soon, we'll be late,' I announced.

'We're in plenty of time, Katie Ann,' said Mum. 'Just be quiet and bring the coats.'

'Auntie's coming ... Auntie's coming ...' chanted Rona.

My tomboy middle-sister Jessie was already outside, scuffing her shoes against the step.

Eagerly we made our way to the pier.

'What did I tell you? You'll have us half-frozen waiting,' said Mum, as the wind did its easterly utmost to strip the skin from our bones. The hull of the *Lochinvar* was a mere speck on the horizon. I shrugged and huddled closer to Rona, watching the approach of the boat, remembering the times I'd spent on board: that first time, when I was only five, sailing to an island I'd never seen before, my mind buzzing with questions. How were islands made? Would there be cows on Mull? How many would we keep? Could I help milk them? ... And then there was that other time, six months ago, when the doctor had sent me to hospital to have my appendix out. What an adventure that had been...!

'The ferry's on its way,' Jessie pointed out, jerking me back to the present.

Sure enough, a small motor boat, full of passengers was crossing the narrow stretch of water between the large boat and the quay.

My heart leapt with excitement.

'There she is!' cried Rona, hopping up and down with delight. Yes, there amongst the familiar local faces was our long-awaited visitor - a comfortable, black-coated figure, complete with walking-stick.

'Auntie Seonaid! Auntie Seonaid! Hello!' I yelled.

The figure waved and proceeded to negotiate the gap between the ferry and the pier like a veteran. Auntie Seonaid (pronounced Shon-id) was next thing to a grandmother to us. She was Mum's aunt, born, like Mum, on the island of Raasay, and even though she had lived in Glasgow for the best part of fifty years, her visits to our isolated home brought a welcome breath of Highland air. Mum would sink into a chair and indulge in reminiscences. Dad would relate hilarious anecdotes from his youth.

As for me, I just loved everything about Auntie Seonaid, from the way her green eyes sparkled when she laughed, to the way they continued twinkling even when she scolded. Oddly enough, no matter how awful I'd been, she was always convinced I'd turn out well, and it was probably this more than anything else that endeared her to me. I couldn't feel her confidence was justified. As soon as her back was turned I would fight with Rona and irritate Mum just as usual - all the same it was reassuring to think someone felt so positive about my future.

That evening, keen to hear more of Dad's stories, I campaigned for permission to stay up late.

'Couldn't we stay this once. Because Auntie Seonaid is here,' I pleaded.

I didn't expect Dad to swallow it (in fact I was fully prepared for an evening spent eaves-dropping with Jessie and Rona on the stairs) but to my amazement, after some initial resistance he agreed.

'All right. Just this once.' Those were his words. I could hardly believe it. Auntie Seonaid had a way with parental authority.

It was a totally hilarious evening. Listening to the three adults talking, I felt as if I was taking part in the very incidents which they described. They had the ability to recount perfectly ordinary events in a manner that had us holding our sides with laughter. And to this very day, I can think of no better form of entertainment.

All too soon the clock struck twelve. Mum looked round meaningfully. It was time for the final bed-time ritual - a Scripture reading from the huge Gaelic Bible on the shelf above Dad's chair. This, according to Mum, with her strict Free Presbyterian upbringing, was the proper way to end the day.

As the most senior member of the household, Auntie Seonaid was asked to choose a suitable passage. I was disappointed when she turned to the second half of the book. She won't get much action there, I thought. As far as I remembered most of the exciting bits - the plagues, battles and suchlike - were located towards the beginning. Resigning myself to boredom, I lay back in the chair and let the melodious flow of language wash over me.

'When the Son of Man shall come in his glory and all his holy angels with him, then shall he sit upon the throne of his glory: And before him shall be gathered all nations: and he shall separate them one from another, as a shepherd divideth his sheep from the goats; And he shall set the sheep on his right hand, but the goats on the left....'

There was more, but after those first few sentences, I
lost interest. My mind wandered and I might have drifted
into a doze had not Auntie Seonaid brought me up short
with a question.

'Now then, Katie Ann, what was that passage about?'

Hey that's not fair, I protested inwardly. Still I'd heard
enough to brazen the thing out.

'It was about animals,' I said.

I saw Dad smiling to himself. Dad wasn't a church-
goer, but he led a good life; a better life, he was quick to
point out than many church-goers of his acquaintance.

'The passage wasn't about animals, it was about
people,' Auntie Seonaid explained carefully. 'About
good people and bad people. The good people are like
sheep and the bad people are like goats, and each of us has
to decide which we're going to be.'

'I'm going to be a nurse,' I said brightly. 'Which is
that?'

At this Mum called a halt to the inquisition. 'Away to
bed now.'

'Good night everyone.' I rose, relieved that I had got
myself out of a sticky situation.

But Auntie Seonaid had the last word. She was on her
feet now, limping across the room to return the Bible to
its niche.

'You'll be a good girl yet, Katie Ann!'

The confident lilt of her prediction chased me up-
stairs.

Cool blustery weather gave way to an unusually fine
September. Dad made hay. Mum made bramble jam.
Jessie and Rona caught the measles and far from becom-

ing a better girl, I brought near-disaster upon the entire household.

It all began when Mum told me for the third time to go and put logs in the *modern mistress* (*modern mistress* was the name shamelessly sported by the ancient black range in our kitchen). I'd ignored her first two requests. With Rona and Jessie still confined to bed, I was making the most of a captive audience, regaling them with everything I'd done in school that day. This third request, however, was more in the nature of an explosion.

'Katie Ann, if you don't go down this minute and put logs on the fire, Dad will be in, the stove will be out, and then there will be a noise!'

'Just let me finish this bit ...' I held out long enough to explain the intricacies of the new stitch I'd learnt in needle-work and then departed.

Downstairs I very much regretted that delay. The stove of the *modern mistress* was full of ash with only a tiny red glow at the centre. In half an hour Mum would be down to make the tea! In a last-ditch attempt to salvage the situation, I stuffed as many logs as would fit through the door and pulled out the damper.

'Was the fire all right?' Mum inquired when I returned to the bedroom.

'Mmm,' I replied, as if the answer was too obvious to require enunciation.

'There's a lot of smoke around,' she remarked some minutes later.

I looked out of the window. 'So there is.' I had a sort of churning feeling in the pit of my stomach - a sense of impending doom. And even as I looked the smoke became denser and blacker, and a foul acrid smell invaded the room.

'Don't tell me you left the damper out!' gasped Mum.

'It wasn't me. It must have been somebody else,' I bleated.

And to think I'd been worried in case Dad arrived home to a cold kitchen! The *modern mistress* was absolutely roasting, while outside a veritable fire-work display of sparks and dramatic orange flames spewed from the chimney.

With a wooden frame under the roof and a barn full of hay, there was every possibility of an almighty conflagration. Mum dashed back into the house and threw salt into the stove. As if from nowhere Dad appeared with a ladder and started frantically ferrying buckets of water up to the roof. He punctuated his descents with threats and furious glares.

'If that byre goes on fire, Katie Ann, you're for it ...'

'If that barn goes up in flames, you won't know what's hit you...'

But Dad's threats were nothing compared to the wail that came from Mum when she looked up at the bedroom window. It would have done a banshee justice.

'Ahh! Those children will catch their deaths and it's all your fault!'

I looked up. There were Jessie and Rona, perched, legs dangling, on the outer window-ledge, clapping their measled little hands in excitement.

Mum made the tea that evening on the less impressive flame of a primus stove, and to my surprise I didn't feel in the least bit guilty. Somehow at the height of the crisis I'd entered into a state of detachment verging on euphoria. Everything was so awful, it simply ceased to matter. Still, deep down, the incident did nothing to bolster my self-esteem.

That had never been high. I didn't need anyone to tell me that I wasn't good-natured like Jessie and Rona. I was impatient and quick-tempered and, to my mind, impossible to love.

'I don't think you love me,' I informed Mum some time later.

'Don't ever say that again, Katie Ann,' she snapped back. 'Of course I love you. Every mother loves her children.'

I wasn't reassured. Looking back now, though, I can see so many evidences of my mother's love; her hard physical work, the self-sacrifice to give us clothes, the hours spent baking oat-cakes, scones and dumplings just because we liked them, and all without the benefit of electricity or running water. Emotionally she was bringing us up to stand on our own two feet - to face hardships in life, to be prepared to handle rejection.

I didn't understand that then, and even if I had, I doubt if it would have made any difference to the way I felt about myself - Katie Ann, the one who didn't quite fit in.

But at least I *did* know what I was going to do when I grew up. Ever since that spell as a patient in Oban Cottage Hospital when I was nine years old, I'd wanted to become a nurse. I told anyone and everyone of my ambition, including, eventually, the Director of Education for the Argyll Education Board, who in turn told me that if I worked hard and passed an exam, I would get a grant to go to a pre-nursing college in Glasgow.

In September 1954, fifteen years old, and with the unbelievable riches of a grant at my disposal, I emerged from West Coast seclusion, enrolled in Logan and Johnson pre-nursing college and went to Glasgow to stay with Auntie Seonaid.

One of the first things I did there was to buy a full-skirted grey and blue dress for Mum and a white shirt with brown stripes for Dad; the only new clothes they'd had in years. The gifts almost overwhelmed them, and, although I'd have been the last to admit it (wishing to maintain my sophisticated city image from the outset) I found the change of life-style pretty overwhelming myself.

But before long it was as if I'd never lived anywhere else. I hopped on and off tram-cars, became addicted to the cinema, made lots of new friends, and attended church. The attending church bit was Auntie Seonaid's idea. Her arthritis now made it impossible for her to go herself, but she packed me off, in my sensible tweed coat and ghastly scone-shaped beret, every Sunday morning without fail.

'Dad and Mum never made me go to church,' I protested to begin with.

'Because there wasn't a proper church for you to go to,' said Auntie Seonaid. 'But you don't have that excuse any more.'

So I went; and the only thing that made the weekly ritual bearable was the sight of handsome, broad-shouldered Angus MacPherson three pews down on the left hand side. We never got much beyond the stage of exchanging sneaky glances during the metrical psalms, but I lived in hope of romantic developments. Daydreaming about him took my mind off the sermon.

'What did the Minister preach about this morning?' Auntie Seonaid would inquire hopefully on my return.

'Och, it was the same old thing: no dancing, no smoking, no pictures, no football.'

A look of disappointment would flit across her face.

'Surely there was more to his message than that?'

'There surely was. He went on at us for over an hour, the old windbag, but I can't remember a word of it.'

How I resented those sermons. It seemed to me that the man deliberately set out to condemn everything I enjoyed. Ceilidhs and dances were sinful. Going to see Showboat was more wicked still. As for Angus, well my romantic fantasies, apparently, were in the fire and brimstone league!

Christianity, I decided, might be a comfort to Auntie Seonaid and the faithful old souls who visited her, but it was nothing but a kill-joy to me. In fact I began to take a perverse delight in being wayward. The very fact that the Minister had denounced something was enough to make me want to give it a go.

'There's a man called Billy Graham conducting an evangelistic crusade in the Kelvin Hall,' I informed Auntie Seonaid over lunch one Sunday.

'Is that so?'

'Yes, the Minister warned us not to have anything to do with him.' I reached for the gravy. 'So what's an evangelistic crusade anyway?'

'Och, something American, I dare say. But you wouldn't be thinking of going when the Minister doesn't approve?'

In fact I had been invited to the crusade by a friend the previous week and had told her I wasn't interested. In the light of the Minister's sermon, however, I now felt that an evangelistic crusade was definitely worth a visit.

'Mmm.' I stuffed my mouth full of potato, so my reply to Auntie Seonaid's question was understandably indistinct.

'This Billy Graham chap sounds really something,' I exclaimed as I got off the tram with Ishbel a couple of days later.

The sight of people queuing right round the side of the hall seemed to confirm this, and by the time the doors opened and we filed into the main body of the auditorium, I was fully expecting a cross between Frank Sinatra and Humphrey Bogart to appear on the platform. It was a big disappointment to discover that Billy Graham was just an ordinary-looking man in an ordinary-looking suit, and I felt totally cheated when he proceeded quietly to open the meeting with prayer.

So what had the Minister been making such a fuss about? There wasn't the faintest whiff of a dance routine! An evangelistic meeting, apparently, was like a Sunday service in the middle of the week with no Angus MacPherson to liven things up, and like a fool, I'd walked into one of my own free will. Kicking myself, I spent the first few minutes estimating the number of people who, presumably, had made a similar mistake.

Before long, though, I'd given up counting heads and started to listen. There was something strangely gripping about the way this soft-spoken American preacher talked about his faith. It was as if he knew God in a special way; and little by little his words were making an impression on me. A bigger impression than anything I'd ever heard before in my whole life. God was so real to him, I began to feel He might become real to me too. It wasn't a comfortable feeling. Glancing across at Ishbel, I saw that, like me, she was drinking in every word.

'So what did you make of that?' I asked her eagerly some two hours later, as we made our way to the tram-halt.

'There was an awful crowd of folks went forward at the end. I never thought there would be that many.'

'No,' I agreed. 'Neither did I. And the wee wifie on the other side of me was crying buckets. Makes you think, doesn't it?'

'You can say that again,' she echoed.

The following afternoon Auntie Seonaid had a formal visit from Margaret MacLeod. There was never any shortage of passers-by dropping into the house for a cup of tea, but only two particular friends gave prior notice. One was Margaret, and the other a lady called Chursty (pronounced Kirsty) Pollock. When either of them was expected, Auntie Seonaid would set two china cups on a snow-white cloth and tuck a fine lace handkerchief up her sleeve. The handkerchief was chiefly for Chursty's benefit, for, like Auntie Seonaid, Chursty was a widow with a single unmarried son, and the two of them enjoyed nothing better than a companionable weep into their respective hankies. With Margaret the conversation tended to be of a more theological nature, so when she came I generally listened with no more than half an ear.

On this occasion, though, I was really interested. The impact of the previous evening had lessened, but I still had an uncomfortable questioning feeling inside. Why was it that church and sermons and Bible reading seemed to mean so much to Auntie Seonaid and to Margaret when they meant so very little to me?

To my surprise I discovered that these two elderly ladies were talking about God in much the same manner as Billy Graham had - as if they were in daily direct contact with Him. It struck me suddenly that this was the reason why, despite constant pain and increasing disability, Auntie Seonaid remained in such glowing good spirits: she really believed God knew about her problems and that His hand was upon her life.

'Auntie Seonaid!' I burst impulsively into the conversation. 'You'll never guess what Billy Graham said last night! He told us that when Jesus died on the cross He paid the penalty for sin and because of that God's salvation is free to anyone who turns from sin and accepts Jesus as their personal Saviour. So what do you make of that?'

I could tell from her expression that her immediate reaction was one of utter amazement that I'd recalled so much of any sermon. She looked at Margaret, took a deep breath and observed: 'That seems like the right thing to me.'

'Yes, that sounds all right,' Margaret agreed.

'Then why did the Minister tell us not to go anywhere near Billy Graham's meetings?' I challenged.

It really wasn't fair to put them in a spot like that. They were such staunch church members and thought so highly of their Minister; but they could still reason things out for themselves.

'In my opinion that Billy Graham is a good man,' Auntie Seonaid pronounced.

'And doing God's work,' Margaret added.

I could have hugged them. They had set my mind at rest and the way forward, though uninviting, was now as clear as a church bell.

'After what I heard last night, I'm going to try to improve,' I vowed. 'I won't go to any more films or dances and I'll read a chapter of my Bible every day.'

'There now, what did I tell you!' Auntie Seonaid

smiled triumphantly. 'You'll finish up a better girl than any of them.'

This time I won't let her down, I thought. I'm going to be different ... I am ... I really am ...

CHAPTER TWO

'DO IT FOR ME, LORD!'

'Now what can I do for you, Katie - it is Katie, isn't it?'
The Minister peered at me over the rim of his spectacles.
'You wanted to speak to me about something, I believe.'

Nervously, I pushed the application form across his
study desk. 'Well, it's about this, actually. I'm applying
to the Royal Infirmary in Inverness and I was wondering
if you'd ...'

'Furnish a reference,' he finished, inspecting me more
closely than ever. 'Well, I can't see any problem about
that.' To my intense relief he reached for his fountain pen.
'You attend church regularly and you have every appearance of being a very good girl. You don't frequent
worldly places such as dance-halls or cinemas, now do
you?'

'Oh no,' I assured him fervently.

'Just as I thought.' He was writing on the form now -
two succinct lines of copperplate. 'There you are, my
dear. God bless you!'

He smiled benevolently and I felt almost sorry for the
awful things I'd said about his sermons.

'Goodbye, my dear.'

'Goodbye and thank you.' I tripped from the room,
only just managing to sustain my angelic pose as far as
the gate. Who would have expected the Minister to be so
obliging? I'd looked over the catechism and prepared

myself for an interview - an interrogation even - lasting at least half an hour; and here I was, outside the lion's den after a mere five minutes. Exultantly I popped the application into the nearest post box and treated myself to a celebratory cup of coffee in town, before dashing home to doll myself up for the dance that evening.

The fact that I'd just told my Minister a bare-faced lie didn't trouble me in the least. I'd long since become reconciled to my unreformed state. For three whole weeks after the Billy Graham crusade meeting I'd stuck to the straight and narrow path and then a new Lucille Ball film had come to the 'Cosmo'. I'd gone to see it. I couldn't stop myself. And the next thing I knew I was heading back to dances and ceilidhs as fast as my feet and public transport would take me. Moreover, I'd come to a decision. It was one thing to mislead the Minister for the sake of a reference, it was another thing to be an out and out hypocrite. The minute I left for Inverness, I had decided, I would drop the sham of church-attendance ... would be my own person ... answerable to no-one but myself.

And finally that happy day dawned. For the first time I walked through the entrance gates of the Royal Northern Infirmary and on into the faintly antiseptic corridors within. The sun was shining and my mood matched the weather. Life felt good. I had passed my preliminary exams and was about to begin my training with a three month spell on (oh joy!) a children's ward. Nothing could have suited me better.

'You're a nurse,' I proudly informed my uniformed reflection in a glass door. 'A real live student nurse!'

This honeymoon feeling lasted precisely two weeks. For two whole weeks I made beds (with meticulous envelope corners!) changed sheets and nappies, emptied potties, washed bottoms and generally did everything asked of me with the best will in the world. Then, during the third week, the Ward Sister told me to feed three-year-old Ronnie Harmen his dinner.

It wasn't a major undertaking. Ronnie was an obliging little fellow and with a couple of spoonfuls for Mummy and a spoonful for Daddy, one for Teddy and three for all the little children who didn't have any, we got the mince and potatoes down nicely. But he point blank refused to open his mouth for vegetables - no, not for anybody, so in the end I gave up trying. Unfortunately Sister spotted me as I was about to scrape his plate into the bin.

'Nurse MacKinnon,' she snapped. 'I expected you to give that child a balanced meal, not just protein and carbohydrate.'

'I'm sorry, Sister,' my natural reaction was to justify myself, 'but he really hates cabbage.'

Ooops! Suddenly I remembered that student nurses did not talk back to their superiors. There was a moment of total silence during which Sister gave me a look that would have melted lead.

'We'll see about that.'

Snatching the plate, she strode over to Ronnie's cot. 'Now then, my little man, I've a pocketful of sweeties here and you shall have one for every mouthful of cabbage you eat. Open up, like a good boy.'

And he did. He ate every rubbery scrap and she proceeded to stuff him with jelly babies. Student nurses, of course, were strictly forbidden to bribe the children, but Sister didn't take that into account.

'You simply didn't try hard enough, Nurse MacKinnon. And to make matters worse, you were insolent!'

From then on, as far as she was concerned, nothing I did was right. I found myself continually being hauled over the coals for things that hadn't even happened when I was on duty. I retaliated by telling all the other nurses exactly what I thought of the hospital authorities and their notions of discipline. Words such as 'unfair', 'tyrannical', 'archaic', and 'petty-minded' littered my conversation, together with a colourful array of expletives. And I backed them up with my actions. When I wanted to go out at night, I stuffed my bed with a couple of pillows and a mop-head in rollers. When Sister bawled me out, I imitated her recklessly behind her back. But in spite of all this, I was never careless about my work. I loved nursing and knew I had the potential to be a good nurse, which made it all the more galling to find myself lumped in the same ability bracket as the student who created chaos on the medical ward by soaking thirty sets of false teeth in one basin without any means of identifying their owners!

After three months I was transferred to the male surgical ward. Although sorry to leave my small patients, anything (even a lengthy spell of night-duty) seemed preferable to working under Sister Stewart. 'I'll begin again,' I decided, as I was introduced to my new Ward Sister. 'I'll win her approval if it's the last thing I do.'

Things improved after that, but although I got on well with that particular Sister, I still seemed to have a natural flair for making enemies amongst my superiors, and I still found plenty to complain about:

'The system stinks! First year nurses are the lowest form of hospital life. Everyone treats us like dirt,' I fumed at a fellow student on my way out of the hospital one evening.

My companion nodded ... but she didn't seem particularly perturbed.

'I mean, take tonight for instance. Here we are, off duty half an hour late. It isn't worth going to the cinema and I couldn't dance if you paid me, my feet are that sore. You would think Sister would be a bit more considerate on a Saturday. But that's the way it is in this place - first year nurses are the last to be considered. I mean, if there was a fire, they'd probably expect us to go up with the building ...'

Still my companion remained irritatingly good-humoured. She was listening to me, but she didn't seem to be taking what I said on board. Perhaps her evening had not been ruined the way mine had.

'So what are you doing tonight anyway?' I inquired.

There was a momentary hesitation, then: 'I'm going to a prayer meeting,' she replied.

You could have knocked me down with a feather. '*A prayer meeting*! You mean a meeting where people sit around and pray! I thought only sixty year-old women did that!'

'Oh no,' she said happily. 'There'll be lots of other young people there.'

She didn't need to tell me she was looking forward to it. I could see that by her face.

'You'll never guess what Jean Sutherland does on Saturday nights, 'I gleefully informed Ann, a nursing friend, as soon as I got back to the Home. 'She goes to a *prayer meeting*!' The news did not have quite the bombshell effect I had hoped. Ann knew already and was able to cap my information.

'So what?' she shrugged. 'She's religious, isn't she? She goes along to the Nurses' Christian Fellowship and what's more, her boyfriend's a doctor here and he's religious too.'

Under normal circumstances this would have made for an interesting discussion: 'What's his name?' 'Where did they meet?' 'How serious is the relationship?' But in this case I let the matter drop. I didn't want to hear any more about Jean than I could help. I had already decided to give her a wide berth in future. Religious friends, to my mind, fell into the same category as walking-sticks and hearing-aids - with any luck I wouldn't be needing one for a good fifty years.

I greeted Jean coolly the following day and made a point of *not* asking how she had enjoyed the prayer meeting. I also made a point of swearing loudly and deliberately any time she came within ear-shot. I wanted her to reveal her true colours, to look shocked and disapproving. But she didn't. She behaved exactly as usual, smiling and quietly going about her work. In the end I found myself watching her with a grudging admiration bordering on envy. This wasn't just because, with her soft dark hair, laughing eyes and quiet competent manner, she was highly attractive and an excellent nurse; there was something about her, some additional quality I couldn't quite put my finger on. 'Peaceableness' was the nearest I could come to describing it. She seemed to live at peace with herself, with the patients and with the rest of the nursing staff. It wasn't that she didn't get her fair share of frustrations, but somehow she usually managed to carry them lightly.

'How do you do it?' I challenged her one morning in the sluice-room. 'How do you manage to stay so cool when your off-duty is changed at the last minute? Don't you ever get mad inside?'

'I do indeed,' she admitted. 'But I try to do my work to please God and I believe that all these things are under His control. That helps me to accept them.'

Her reply sounded convincing enough, but working to please God was a new thought to me. Deep down I wanted to know more. Above all I wanted to find out what made Jean loveable. That was the thing I envied most. People seemed to respond so warmly to her - nurses as well as patients. Maybe if everyone loved me I would be a peaceable person too, I thought. It's easy not to mind what people say when most of the time they're being complimentary.

I continued to make myself as objectionable as possible when Jean was around. But instead of taking the hint and ignoring me, she was as friendly as ever; and then one day, a few weeks later, she invited me to the Nurses' Christian Fellowship.

'My cousin's speaking this evening,' she explained, 'I thought you might like to come along.'

To a Christian fellowship! The idea appealed to me about as much as the toothache. And yet such was the power of Jean's gentle non-judgemental approach that I found myself agreeing to go.

I sat beside her one row from the front and wondered what I had let myself in for. At one point a young doctor came in, made his way to a seat, and smiled across at us; a friendly unassuming smile.

'That's George,' Jean whispered in my left ear.

'I'd guessed,' I said. 'Who's the bloke beside him?'

'David Paterson - the speaker.'

With the meeting about to begin, there was no time for further introductions. The young man beside George had risen to his feet and stood before us, an open Bible in his hands. As soon as he opened his mouth I recognized the reality of God in his life. Like Billy Graham, David Paterson seemed to have 'arrived' spiritually and his words had a similar penetrating power. He spoke about the judgement of God.

'I've taken my text from the book of Isaiah,' he began and there was a flurry of paper as nurses all around me leafed through their Bibles.

'And in mercy shall the throne be established: and he shall sit upon it ... judging and seeking judgement ...'

David read the words slowly and then explained how Jesus would one day judge the nations from His throne. This came as no surprise. Had not Auntie Seonaid said exactly the same thing? But David went on to explain that Christ's throne was not just a throne of judgement, it was a throne of mercy as well.

This was a new idea as far as I was concerned, but I did not find it particularly reassuring. That throne might be a throne of mercy for people like him and Jean and Auntie Seonaid, but for me it could only be a throne of judgement, I thought. I was under no illusions about my spiritual condition. In my mind's eye, God was a God of the clenched fist, poised to consign me to hell for swearing and smoking and a hundred other sins. To put it in Auntie Seonaid's terms, I was a goat not a sheep and I knew it.

'So what's your definition of a Christian anyway?' I cornered Jean rather belligerently in the sluice-room some weeks later.

'Hmmm,' thoughtfully she propped her slender frame against the sterilizer, 'according to Scripture, a Christian is someone who has been born again spiritually.'

'And what happens to people who *haven't* been born again spiritually when they die?'

'The Bible teaches that only those who have received Jesus as their Saviour and have His Spirit living within them, will share His glory,' she said.

Two things struck me. In the first place I realized Jean wasn't just giving me her own opinion. Everything she said was based on the Bible. And at the same time it dawned on me how little I knew about the Bible myself. Something of this realization must have showed on my face for the next thing I knew, Jean was suggesting a get-together with George that evening. 'He's much better at explaining things than I am,' she assured me.

'Nurse MacKinnon!' Before I had time to dream up a suitable excuse, our conversation was cut short. As usual it was me Sister was yelling for, not Jean!

'Oh ... all right, 'I muttered. 'Quick, out of my way!' And grabbing a basin, I charged back to work.

When I eventually came off duty at 8.30 p.m. that evening, Jean was waiting for me in the corridor.

'I sent a note to George,' she said. 'We are to meet him in the chapel at nine o'clock.'

I hadn't the heart to disappoint her. I suppose underneath I was amazed and rather touched by her concern for my spiritual welfare. In any case, I *did* have a number of questions...

But seated in the hospital chapel some forty minutes later, my courage was failing rapidly.

'There's no point in hanging about here any longer,' I muttered to Jean. 'Either your note has ended up with a pile of dirty sheets in some laundry basket or your doctor friend has got it and can't be bothered to come.'

'Please, Katie, let's give him another five minutes,' Jean pleaded, peering anxiously up the corridor. 'Oh look! There he is now.'

I looked. Right at the bottom of the corridor I saw a figure racing towards us, white coat flapping out behind. I experienced a fleeting glow of satisfaction, but by the time George had panted into the seat beside us, I had decided I was not in the mood for a religious discussion after all.

'This is pointless. I don't really need to talk to anyone. I mean, it isn't as if I've got problems,' I informed him, scanning his face for signs of resentment at being dragged along miles of corridor on a wild goose-chase. But apparently he was cast in the same imperturbable mould as Jean. He did not seem even mildly taken-aback by my attitude.

'That's fine,' he said. 'Jean just mentioned you wanted to know a bit more about Christianity.'

'Not really.' I tried to sound as off-hand as possible. 'I mean, I would like to be a Christian like Jean, but I can't, so there's no point in discussing it.'

'Why can't you?' George prompted gently.

'I just can't. For one thing, I don't want to give up going to dances and parties.'

George nodded and then almost took my breath away by saying: 'You know, Katie, you can accept Jesus as Saviour, and if you still want to go to dances and parties after that, there is nothing to stop you.'

This was such a novel idea, I simply did not know how to respond. My mind did a double-take and George continued to explain in the same gently authoritative manner that becoming a Christian was a positive, not a negative thing - a matter of getting to know Jesus personally.

This actually made sense. After all, I had noticed myself that Billy Graham and Auntie Seonaid and Mar-

garet MacLeod all seemed to have some special sort of
relationship with God, but now I deliberately looked
blank, as if I had not understood a word he'd been saying.
To my disgust, instead of giving up, George extracted a
well-worn Bible from his pocket.

'Of course what I've been telling you about God's
plan of salvation is all in here,' he said, flipping the book
open on his knee.

The last thing I wanted was a scriptural bombardment
at half past nine in the evening.

'I know,' I interrupted. 'I read it all the time.'

'That's good. What part do you read most?'

I smiled exultantly, convinced I'd got the upper hand
at last. 'The twenty-third psalm - in Gaelic!' I replied.

George didn't bat an eyelid. 'This Bible's in English,
I'm afraid, but we can take a look at the twenty-third
psalm anyway.'

He read the first few verses, then paused. 'The psalm-
ist says here that the Lord is his shepherd. Could you say
that, Katie?'

His eyes searched my face, and when I failed to reply,
he elaborated slightly, explaining how the Lord Jesus had
died for my sin and risen again, and was now a living
shepherd able to lead me along paths of righteousness
and on into eternal life.

As he spoke something rather amazing happened. It
was as if a light went on in my mind. Jesus Himself
seemed to come into the chapel, a shepherd with arms
out-stretched to receive me. My whole attitude changed
- even my face looked different, Jean told me afterwards.
Suddenly I was as eager as a home-sick child to respond
to the love that had taken this Saviour to Calvary for my
sake.

'Please, pray with me, George,' I whispered.

Jean took my hand and George prayed - a simple prayer asking Jesus to come into my life.

And He did. At that moment I experienced the new birth Jean had spoken of in the sluice-room that morning. I knew it as surely as I have ever known anything. God's Holy Spirit came into my heart. For the first time in my life I felt loved and accepted from the top of my head to the tip of my toes. 'I can't believe it! I can't believe it!' I marvelled, laughing, crying and throwing my arms round Jean all at the same time. She was crying too and the smile on George's face would have melted an igloo.

When, over half an hour later, we finally left the chapel in deference (unusual for me!) to hospital regulations, I went straight back to my room and hunted out a Bible. Huddled with a torch under the blankets, I started reading.

And here, if I'd needed it, was further confirmation of the spiritual change that had taken place. The words meant something to me. I recognized Jesus, *my* Lord and Saviour, walking through the pages of the gospels. I read ... and read ... and eventually, having feasted almost until dawn on this vision of a love that promised to accept me warts and all, I fell asleep on top of my torch, my Bible still open beside me on the pillow.

Almost without realizing it, I had taken the first infant steps of faith. Looking back, I recognize God's hand in all the circumstances which brought me to that point. I also recognize that not every Christian will have an instantaneous conversion similar to my own. For some coming to faith in Christ is a gradual process. Others may receive Him at such an early age, they can scarcely remember a time when they have not been conscious of His presence and, as adults, they build upon this childhood commitment. But true conversion, whether it takes place instantaneously or over a period of years, is always the work of the Holy Spirit. And, having repented of sin and received God's gift of salvation, it is the power of the indwelling Spirit that enables us to conquer sin day by day.

In the wake of the Billy Graham Crusade, I had discovered the futility of trying to curb my natural desires in my own strength. Now, in the wake of my experience in the hospital chapel, I discovered what a difference it made to know Jesus personally. I woke up next morning feeling free and joy-filled as never before. When Jean suggested meeting each day for prayer and Bible reading, I was delighted. A spiritual hunger had taken the place of my previous hunger for entertainment.

In the weeks that followed, I did not consciously deny myself anything; I simply found that learning about Jesus was one hundred times more satisfying than going to the pictures. All I wanted to do in my spare time was read the Bible and discuss aspects of the Christian faith with Jean. Again, without making any conscious effort, I stopped swearing. And I started to enjoy church. 'To think I once thought this was for pensioners! Becoming a Christian has completely changed the way I feel,' I told Jean exuberantly after the service one Sunday.

'That's good, but it's important not to rely too much on feelings,' she warned me. 'Faith is about trusting God and believing His word whether you feel like it or not.'

'I know,' I nodded. But underneath I found it impossible to conceive how anyone could know Jesus and not wake up each morning feeling as if the whole world had been redecorated.

Inevitably the bubble burst. After six weeks on an unbroken spiritual high, I suddenly realized I wasn't in any danger of sprouting wings. I found myself in church one Sunday with nothing to put on the collection plate. The last of my pay packet had gone on cigarettes the previous day.

'Do you think it's wrong for me to smoke?' I asked Jean next morning.

'Why? Has someone been lecturing you?' she inquired. (I later discovered she had expressly forbidden the other Christian nurses to say anything.)

'No. I just wondered.'

At this Jean considered me thoughtfully. 'If you think God is speaking to you about smoking, you just go and ask Him whether He wants you to give it up.'

I followed her advice and concluded that He did.

'Lord, this will be tough, but for Your sake I'll do it,' I vowed. And the battle began. As much as anything else my Christian witness was at stake, I felt. There had been a generally incredulous reaction amongst the hospital staff to the news of my conversion. Giving up smoking would be an opportunity to show them I meant business. I took the bit between my teeth and cut down to two cigarettes a day.

'This time next week I'll have kicked the habit completely,' I informed the nurses at the Christian fellowship meeting.

But the following Monday everything went wrong. For the first time since the night in the chapel, I had a major row with Sister, and was back to square one, smoking like a chimney.

'Don't tell me you're going to let yourself be beaten by a tiny thing like a cigarette,?' a Christian doctor tried to bolster my flagging spirits.

'Of course not,' I said miserably. I still loved God and longed to glorify Him. But, in the weeks that followed, the more I tried to have an effective Christian witness, the more I wanted to smoke. I studied my Bible and prayed and went to Church as regularly as ever, but I kept sneaking into the toilets for a quick drag. I hated myself for it. The compulsion seemed to tarnish everything. Try as I would, I could not give it up.

Eventually, in desperation, I went to see George.

'Stop trying in your own strength, Katie. Ask the Lord to give you His,' he advised.

By this stage I would have done anything, no matter how feeble it seemed. I went back to my room and knelt beside my bed. 'Jesus, You know I believe You want me to stop smoking, but somehow I just can not manage it,' I prayed. 'So please, will You do it for me?'

I stood up, took my cigarettes and matches and burned them in the yard. Then I came back to my room, washed the walls and flung open the windows. The battle was over. My craving for cigarettes had gone completely, never to return. Moreover I had learned an invaluable spiritual lesson; it underlay the whole of my Christian experience up to that point, I realized, and gave me confidence for the future. Despite the many faults which I now knew to be still part of my character, God was supernaturally able to do in me the things I could not do for myself.

CHAPTER THREE

CHOICES

My conversion held a special significance for Jean and George. They had been seeking God's will for their future, and the fact that He had used them jointly to lead me to Christ set the seal on their relationship. Before long they shared an important secret with me.

'We're hoping to get married after I sit my finals,' said Jean, her eyes sparkling with excitement, 'and I want you to be one of the bridesmaids.'

I was delighted for them, even though, at that stage, I was not particularly struck on the idea of marriage myself. As far as I could see wives were the ones who made all the effort and husbands only considered them when they had nothing more pressing on their minds.

'But Katie,' George would protest, 'Look at Paul's teaching in Ephesians 5. Husbands are to love their wives as Christ loved the Church. That does not leave any room for selfishness.'

Easter rolled round and with it the wedding - one of the happiest I had ever attended. Jean looked radiantly beautiful in her white dress, while we bridesmaids stood by her side in pink, and modestly tripped our way through compliments.

'I dare say the next Big Day will be your own,' a jovial guest teased. Automatically I treated him to my standard reply: 'Not on your life! Men are self-opinionated, demanding and selfish. A husband is the last thing I want.'

He looked rather offended ... of course I hadn't *intended* him to take it personally ... but that was the worst of having a big mouth, strong opinions, and a short memory. Over the months, George and Jean had been doing their best to help me come to a more balanced understanding of what Christian marriage was about, but I still kept losing sight of the Scriptural principles, and I still hadn't completely lost the idea that I was the unlovable type.

I missed Jean a great deal when she left Inverness. Fortunately, though, I could still visit her parents' home on my days off, and they were an immense help to me spiritually. Jean, herself, was an excellent correspondent. As the months passed I began to write to her more and more about the future. What should I do when I finished my training? Two main considerations dominated my thoughts: I wanted to get somewhere in my chosen career, and I wanted to grow spiritually. The two went hand in hand, I believed, for I felt sure God had called me to nursing and it seemed I could serve Him best by becoming a thoroughly competent nurse.

For this I needed experience and further qualifications. Accordingly, I accepted the post of staff nurse in a hospital in Greenock, welcoming from the word 'go' the additional responsibility which it entailed. The attendant spiritual challenge, however, was another matter. With Jean now expecting her first baby in Glasgow and her parents equally far away in Inverness, I found myself spiritually propless, forced, for the first time, to rely solely on God for day to day support. It was by no means easy, but then such growth-periods rarely are; I perse-vered through the lonely patches and emerged with fresh confidence in my Lord's ability to keep me walking in His will.

Then it was back to inner city Glasgow for a period of midwifery training. This proved in many ways to be one of the happiest times in my nursing career. Not only was I near to Jean, George and baby Alison, but the work, though demanding, was very fulfilling. At that time pupil midwives were required to do thirty home deliveries. We had minimal equipment. The experience was to prove unimaginably valuable to me and the first cry of a new-born infant never ceased to thrill me to the core. As for the people - I found them totally refreshing. Where but in Glasgow could I have had the experience of knocking on the door of a tenement 'single end' (one room for the whole family!) to be greeted by a naked man holding a strategically placed cushion in front of him, and of then being matter-of-factly led over to a bed to examine his wife and newly born child? Nobody stood on their dignity. And this general unselfconsciousness was cou-pled with a wonderful sense of fun.

And what a privilege it was to be near Auntie Seonaid in the months before she died! She was confined to bed by this stage, suffering from cancer, but the door was always open for callers. Her greeting was as bright and her faith as strong as ever. When she died I contemplated afresh the joy for a Christian of going to be with Jesus in heaven. I visualized her eternally free from pain in the presence of her Saviour and knew that one day I would see her again.

It was around this time I came across someone who made a strong impression on me. Jan Walkinshaw had

just finished Bible School and had come to the Royal
Maternity to do midwifery training before going out to
Tanzania to work as a missionary with the Africa Inland
Mission. Initially I was intrigued by the contrast between
her youthful face and her striking white hair, but soon I
found myself remarking on her faith. She knew that God
had called her to serve Him as a missionary nurse and was
trusting Him to supply the money for her fare to Tanzania. How we rejoiced when that money, all £200 of it (a
vast sum in those days) was handed into the Bible School
by an anonymous donor. 'Mind you,' I told her afterwards, 'I'm glad God is not calling me to Bible School
and missionary work, because I could not possibly leave
nursing.'

To my discomfiture she looked me straight in the eye.

'Don't be too sure of that,' she said.

What did she mean? What a ridiculous suggestion!
Stop nursing and go to Bible College! God couldn't
possibly want me to do that - or could he?

The seed of doubt had been sown. I fought its growth.
The last thing I wanted to do was heed the prompting of
a faint yet persistent inner voice. And yet, in the end, I
could ignore it no longer. I sat down and wrote a letter to
Mr. MacBeath, the Principal of the Bible Training Insti-
tute in Glasgow.

Almost by return of post I had my reply. Would I be
free to attend an interview the following week?

When the day came, I felt strangely detached from the
whole proceedings - almost as if they were happening to
somebody else. Mr. MacBeath called me into his office.

'Why do you want to come to Bible College?' he
asked.

'I don't want to come,' I said glumly.

He looked rather puzzled . 'Oh, I'm sorry. There must be some mistake. I thought I was interviewing you as a potential student.'

'You are, unfortunately,' I replied. 'But I'm not here because *I* want to be. I would much rather stay in nursing. It's just that I've got a horrible feeling coming here is God's will.'

Ooops, had I put my foot in it again? This, surely, was not the way to speak to the principal of a world-famous Bible College. But to my relief, Mr. MacBeath seemed more amused than anything else. 'Ah, yes,' he said. 'I see what you mean.'

And so I became a student at B.T.I. and began very tentatively to think in terms of missionary service. Since the interview had taken place in January and my course did not begin until September it seemed sensible to take a course on tropical diseases in the interim. Secretly, though, I still hoped the Lord was sending me to Bible College simply to learn more about the Bible and that afterwards I would be free to return to the work I dearly loved - nursing.

In fact, Bible College turned out to be much more fun than I expected. Perhaps 'fun' is the wrong word. There was, of course, a profoundly serious side to life; day by day I sat at the feet of spiritual leaders, learning not just from their extensive knowledge of the Scriptures, but from their proven experience of God. Every lecture started with a prayer and we were continually challenged to put Scriptural principles into practice in our everyday lives. At the same time, with a 160 strong Christian community in residence, Bible College also lent itself to heart-to-heart chats over coffee, to crazy pranks (such as attaching a dried herring to a hidden central heating pipe in the room of the most fastidious member of our community), and to getting to know people the way they really were, at their best and at their worst.

This informal, social side of life was every bit as important to my spiritual development as the formal study side. I was forced to revise some strongly-held opinions. I met Christian girls who wore lip-stick! - up to this stage I had held very rigid views on the sinfulness of make-up - and who were manifestly more loving and joyful in their walk with the Lord than I was. More astonishing still, I met young Christian men who totally failed to conform to my ideas of chauvinism. I got to know some of them very well and it was like suddenly being presented with half-a-dozen easy-going yet genuinely caring brothers.

And for a while, it even looked as if I might have met Mr. Right. Stephen (I'll call him that) and I had got on well from the first moment we met. We talked and corresponded with one another regularly (he was not a student at the College) and I began to feel that I was falling in love for the first time in my life. Then, as suddenly as it began, the relationship ended, bringing a great deal of hurt and pain to us both.

Yes, it was an emotional set-back. Old ideas of being unlovable started pushing themselves into my thoughts. But now the knowledge of God's love was there to counterbalance them. The months went by. I felt angry. I felt sorry for myself. Still, He continued to lead me through all the bitterness and confusion, until, eventually peace came, bringing with it the grace which would help me forgive and forget.

By this stage I was into the second year of my course at B.T.I. Each week a missionary home on leave or a representative of one of the many different missionary societies would address the students. Listening to what they had to say, I felt more and more convinced that God was calling me to serve him overseas. I also recognized that my attitude to marriage had changed. A husband was no longer the *last* thing I wanted. At the same time, I had learnt enough from my course and read enough missionary books to dispel any illusions I might have had about marriage prospects on the mission field. I knew that while there were very many single women serving in that capacity there were very few single men. The knowledge did not trouble me unduly. To marry or not to marry? Through all the tears and heart-searching surrounding the break-up of my relationship with Stephen a battle had been fought and won. God had made me content, I felt, for one state or the other.

Full of enthusiasm, I approached my denominational missionary society about the possibility of working as a missionary nurse in Peru. The way ahead seemed clear. God had given me nursing experience, had put me through Bible College and was now giving me the privilege of service overseas. But after a rather unsatisfactory interview and an eighteen-month wait (that nearly drove me crazy), I received word from the Mission Board that my services would not be required. New government regulations in Peru were causing insurmountable problems, and the society had decided to discontinue their medical work. The news was a blow. So much for my missionary call! I'd evidently misread God's will, I concluded, smarting yet again under a sense of rejection. All I could do was pick up the pieces of a confusing experience and carry on.

I decided to visit an aunt in the States. After spending

eighteen months in Providence, Rhode Island, amongst
friendly Americans who seemed fascinated by all things
Scottish, especially my accent, I returned to Glasgow to
work as a Sister in the labour ward of a women's hospital.

I was still there when the law concerning abortion was
liberalized. By this stage I was actually living with Jean
and George, in a basement flat in their home. George,
though as unassuming as ever, was now a consultant.

'There's a Conscience Clause in the Act,' he explained to me. 'No doctor or nurse can be pressurized into
taking part in a procedure to which they have a moral
objection.'

I promptly informed the doctors at the hospital that on
no account would I have anything to do with induced
abortions. Of the many things that I felt strongly about,
this issue came high on the list. In my eyes it was
equivalent to murder; the deliberate murder of the smallest, weakest, most defenceless members of society. Every
part of me revolted against the idea: on moral, on
theological, and also I admit, with my instinctive love for
babies, on strong emotional grounds.

There were a few raised eyebrows, but my position
seemed generally accepted. Some time later, however, I
was asked to assist with a minor, routine operation. 'A
straightforward D and C,' I was told. To my horror, half-
way through, a tiny, perfectly-formed baby was removed
from the womb. Without a moment's hesitation I took off
my gloves and walked out of the theatre, bringing the
nursing staff with me.

The ensuing row culminated in the Hospital Administrator calling a meeting with all the medical staff,
including Matron, and summoning me to give an account
of my actions.

I'll never forget the half-hour I spent before that row of pointedly disapproving faces: 'You put a patient's life at risk,' I was informed.

Fortunately, I wasn't the type to be easily intimidated.

'Wrong,' I retorted, '*You* put the patient at risk, by involving me in a procedure which I consider to be wicked, immoral and offensive to God. It was murder, you know - the murder of a tiny person made in His image, and no scientific clap-trap is going to convince me differently.'

Needless to say this went over like a lead balloon. The faces now registered shocked embarrassment as well as disapproval. George and Jean had already tried to impress upon me the need, while making my point, to be gracious about it, but in those days graciousness just wasn't my style.

I was asked if I wished to resign.

'I'll only go if you fire me,' I said. For the sake of the nurses junior to me I felt at that point it was vital to stick to my guns, even though I *was* keeping something under my cap.

It seemed I had called their bluff. There was no question of dismissal, the Chief Administrator demurred. The meeting had been convened with a view to reaching a mutual understanding. I had made my position clear and in future I would not be required to assist with abortions. As far as he was concerned, the matter was settled.

I do not suggest that I rode out of the affair like a knight in shining armour. Another person, no doubt, could have made the case against abortion far better and handled the whole unhappy business more sensitively than I. At the same time it did seem that God had me there for a purpose. I had set a precedent. From then on it was easier for junior nurses with convictions similar to my own, to stand out against the system, and perhaps a few people were jolted into recognizing that a human foetus could not be equated with an inflamed appendix to be discarded as a matter of convenience.

What my superiors did not know, because in the middle of such a furore, I had not felt it appropriate to tell them, was that I was about to resign anyway - not because I felt forced to, or even because I particularly wanted to, but because God had finally made it clear that I was to serve Him elsewhere.

It had happened in the way such things usually do - unexpectedly. I was genuinely content with my lot; living with George and Jean, acting as an on-call Auntie to Alison, Dorothy, David and George, organising the Nurses Christian Fellowship, and visiting Mum and Dad. I had no desire for a change of life-style, but, out of the blue, a letter from an old friend from Bible College days had set the ball rolling.

That friend's name was Nettie. Like Jan Walkinshaw, she had gone to work with the Africa Inland Mission after leaving B.T.I., and her letter had come from the Mission Hospital in Kijabe, Kenya. She began by apologizing for having taken such an age to get round to writing. She had been busy, she explained, incredibly busy. In fact she was working an average of eighteen hours a day, six days a week.

The labour ward had been particularly slack that day, and I had spent my time knitting. Somehow the two things just didn't add up. Here was my friend about to collapse with exhaustion, while I twiddled six ounces of angora around my index finger. Struck by what seemed a very unfair distribution of labour, I scribbled a hasty note - 'How would you like me to come and give you a hand?' - and posted it next morning.

It was some months before Nettie replied, and this time she made no apologies. The delay had been deliberate. She had wanted to give me time, she explained, to sort out in my own mind whether my offer had been mere impulse, or something more concrete. She concluded by saying that there was certainly a need for someone with my qualifications in Kijabe, and that if I felt it was God's will for me to come, I should get in touch with the Mission Office in London.

Until then it hadn't entered my head to consider anything more than an informal visit, but now Nettie's suggestion seemed like a sensible idea. I wrote to Tom Lloyd, the British General Secretary of A.I.M. explaining that I would like to help Nettie, but was unsure whether it was God's will or not. I told him of my earlier call to missionary work and subsequent disappointment. He wrote back promptly and encouragingly, urging me to keep praying about the possibility of working with the Africa Inland Mission.

And gradually, as I prayed and as Mr. Lloyd continued to give me his support, writing to me every few weeks to assure me of *his* prayers, everything clicked into place. Circumstances, my Bible reading, the advice of trusted Christian friends - all seemed to point in the same direction. God was calling me to Africa ...

'We will aim to pray in your support and have you out there by the autumn,' the Scottish Chairman told me at our introductory meeting.

I was scandalized. 'But Mr. Ross, that's months away!'

The Lord has always had difficulty impressing upon me the value of patience. Still, it was both humbling and reassuring to look back over the years, and see His guiding hand where previously I had only seen my own confusion. I had left Bible College in 1966, expecting to follow through immediately on my missionary call. When things hadn't worked out, I had been bitterly disappointed. But now, six years later, God was revealing the next step of the way. I had not mistaken His call after all. I had simply misjudged His timing.

Things were happening at last! Fortunately, though, the built-in checks of the missionary processing system kept me in Scotland long enough to get my affairs properly sorted out. They also gave me time, once the first flush of enthusiasm had faded slightly, to count the cost of the step I was about to take.

As an A.I.M. missionary I would have no worldly security. I would be trusting God to meet my needs, asking Him to cause people to donate enough money to the Mission each year, to cover my monthly allowance.

'You're crazy!' one of my staff nurses exploded when she heard about this policy. 'Imagine giving up a Sister's post and your lovely wee flat to live like that! Why, you probably won't have enough money to buy yourself *talcum powder*!'

Up to that moment I had been fairly unconcerned about the provision of material things. Of *course* God would provide for me, I had assumed. But now a hint of doubt crept into my mind. At Bible College I had heard countless personal testimonies to the seemingly miraculous way He had supplied the needs of various missionary speakers.

But I saw them as spiritual giants. Was it not the

height of presumption to assume that God would specifically provide something as ordinary as talc for someone as ordinary as me?

This question continued to trouble me on the way to the canteen half-an-hour later.

'Hey, Katie!' As I passed the maternity ward, a nurse I knew slightly, called me aside and thrust a package into my hands. 'I heard you were leaving. This is for you.'

The package contained a bar of *Blue Grass* soap and a tin of talcum powder!

As far as I was concerned that small incident spoke volumes. Through a tin of talc, of a much better quality than anything I would ever have bought for myself, it seemed as if God was pledging not only to meet my intimate personal needs, but to meet them *abundantly*. And that wasn't the end of the matter. I went out to Kenya with a further *twenty-five* tins of talc in my suit-case. So many people gave the stuff to me, I was almost afraid I'd give rise to a national shortage!

But at the end of the day, when the boxes were packed and the good-byes had been said, even in the face of such evidence of God's loving care, I found it terribly hard to leave my family.

It wasn't as if I was just going for a year or two. Initially I had considered that, but the Lord had showed me very clearly that I was to apply for a long-term appointment. I had seen the troubled look on Mum's face and known what was on her mind. She was wondering why I could not be normal like Jessie and Rona and stay at home and get married.

I wondered the same thing myself. To marry or not to marry? On the very brink of my departure, I realized that this was an issue which had not, after all, been settled fully. I faced up to the fact that I had no desire to remain single; that what I really wanted was a home and family of my own.

I prayed about this, hoping for reassurance. With God *everything* was possible; but in place of reassurance, I met with a challenge.

'Are you willing to remain single for My sake, Katie?' my Lord seemed to ask.

How wonderful if I could have joined the ranks of those who freely and joyfully abandoned themselves body, mind and spirit, to His eternal purposes. All I could manage was a whispered variation on the 'Do it for me!' theme:

'Make me willing to be willing, Lord,' I said.

CHAPTER FOUR

THE ADVENTURE BEGINS

With a thunderous roar of engines, the plane swept down the run-way. Faster and faster it travelled, hurtling along the tarmac, to lift and soar like a huge metal bird ... up ... up ...

I sucked furiously on a boiled sweet and peered through the cabin window, savouring my final view of London - a fairy-tale vision of twinkling golden lights. 'I'm off! I'm actually off to Kenya!' I marvelled. After all the emotional upheaval of the preceding weeks, it was as if a huge weight was lifting from my shoulders. Gratefully I remembered all the friends who were praying for me. So many people in so many different church congregations had given me their support. There was the congregation of St. Vincent Street, my own home church, who had promised to pray for me and to contribute towards my allowance. Then there were the folks in Sandyford, George and Jean's church. They, too, would be remembering me week by week at their Saturday night prayer-meeting; and, of course, there were the Mission personnel. I owed so much to their patience and understanding. Thanks to their efforts, I now had a clear idea (in theory) of what being a missionary nurse with A.I.M. was all about.

The primary motivation, as Mr. Lloyd had told me at one of our earliest meetings, was obedience. I had joined a Mission whose main aim was to obey Christ's command to go into all the world and make disciples from every nation, that is, from every group of people who have a language and customs of their own.

'Although we do some relief work, we are first and foremost an evangelistic organisation,' Mr. Lloyd had explained. 'Our aim is to establish churches amongst people as yet unreached by the gospel, and to help established churches to grow.'

So where did nursing fit in, I had asked him?

A missionary nurse, I was told, would probably find herself treating patients who were not Christians and would have the opportunity to speak to them about Christ. Also, she would be helping to train local people to work in the hospital.

This made sense. But as the huge Boeing 707 cut through the night, winging me towards my new role, I couldn't help wondering how it would work out for me in practice. Mr. Lloyd and the Mission Council had seemed so certain I had the makings of a missionary. How awful if I let them down! Still, there was no point in worrying. Already the heat and muffled roar of the engines were having a numbing effect on my thought-processes. It was a relief just to be able to sink back in my seat and relax. For the next seven hours nobody would be expecting anything of me. I kicked off my shoes, shut my eyes - just for a moment! - and slept.

Six hours later I came round sufficiently to raise the blind on the window at my elbow and look out. An awe-inspiring sight met my eyes. To my right the first shimmering rays of day-light streaked across a cloudless violet sky, while thousands of feet below me I could see land - a vast expanse of reddish earth broken by the sinuous strip of a river. My heart skipped a beat. This was Africa - that mysterious, incredibly complex continent, about which, as yet, I knew so little.

A smiling stewardess served breakfast. Gratefully, I sipped my coffee, thinking how different this journey must have been for the first A.I.M. missionaries; those five men and three women, who, over seventy-five years ago, had travelled by sea to Mombasa, to begin their 250 mile trek inland. Whatever would they, and the intrepid men and women who followed them have made of a missionary like me, zooming straight into Kenya in a luxury aircraft? There was no doubt about it, *they* were the stuff that martyrs are made of.

'We are reaping the fruit of their labour to this day,' Tom Lloyd had told me. 'They laid the foundation and established the principles on which we build, and, praise God, over the past three quarters of a century, the Mission has expanded enormously. Churches have been established and thousands have come and are coming to faith in Christ. Mind you, though, we have made our mistakes.'

I knew what he meant. Despite their great courage and dedication, missionaries in the past had tended to mishandle the culture factor. Often their attitude towards African people had smacked of paternalism and little respect had been shown for African values and customs. Times had changed. The Mission was now very conscious of the need to free the gospel from the trappings of Western culture. In 1971 it had turned all its properties over to the National Church and submitted to the authority of national leaders. African leaders were now largely responsible for assigning missionaries to their various positions of service within the church and they could request the removal of any missionary who, in their eyes, did not seem to be making a helpful contribution.

'Ladies and Gentlemen, we are about to commence our descent into Nairobi. Please ensure that your seat-belts are fastened.'

The stewardess's announcement broke in upon my musings. 'This is it!' I thought. The journey was almost over. I was about to land at Kenyatta airport. Suddenly, as I clicked my safety-belt shut, a horrible thought struck me. What if no-one had come to the airport to meet me? Of course the Mission knew I was coming, and I had also been in touch with Ruth Melville, a friend from Bible College. But what if the Mission had got the dates mixed up? And what if my letter to Ruth had gone astray?

Rather anxiously I left the plane, retrieved my suit-cases from baggage-control and made my way through customs.

'Have you anything to declare, Madam?' a white-suited airport official inquired politely.

'Only these.' I laid two pairs of shorts and a couple of tee-shirts on the desk. They were a gift for Ruth's little boy.

'For these you pay,' the official informed me.

'But ... I can't!' I was panic-stricken. 'You see I don't have any Kenyan currency. I might be able to get some, though. I am nearly sure someone is waiting out there to meet me. Is it all right if I take a look?'

The official nodded and I dashed out into the arrivals lounge. To my relief there at the front of the waiting crowd I spotted a familiar figure - a young woman with jet black hair, wearing a blue dress. Ruth had come.

'Oh Ruth,' I blurted, without even taking the time to greet her properly. 'Will you lend me some money? I've brought some little clothes for Andy, but I can't get them through customs without paying duty.'

Ruth took me soothingly by the arm, and led me back to the customs desk.

'Jambo, Bwana, now what have you been telling my friend here?' I was amazed at the ease with which she engaged the official in conversation. The pair of them chatted away in Swahili for a good five minutes until finally he looked in my direction.

'Why did you not tell me that you were bringing these small things as a gift for this lady's boy?' he said, smiling broadly, and with a benevolent sweep of his hand, waved me and my baggage through to the arrivals lounge.

I suppose if I had been in an analytical frame of mind, this incident might have taught me something about the supreme importance Africans place upon relationships. As it was, I was feeling much too hot and too relieved to be analytical. I just hoped with all my heart that I would soon be able to speak Swahili as well as Ruth.

Justy, an A.I.M. missionary who worked in the hospital laboratory had also come to the airport to meet me. Ruth introduced us, and, as we set off for town, Justy explained that we would be living together to begin with, in the house she shared with Sylvia, the hospital Matron. Once I had settled in, though, the plan was for me to move into a place of my own.

I digested this news with a sense of satisfaction. Being sociable by nature, a home of my own, where I could entertain friends, was very important to me. Somehow I felt instinctively that this was the way to get to know African people; to visit them in their homes and to encourage them to drop in with me in mine.

The rest of the day passed in a haze of colour and

conversation. Ruth drove me past glorious beds of pink
and purple bougainvillea and rows of blue flowering
jacaranda trees, into the city, with its modern slate-grey
buildings. There, we visited the A.I.M. office and drank
tea with Norman Thomas, the Kenyan Field Representative and his wife.

'We've arranged for you to travel up to Kijabe tomor-
row, after you have registered with the Nursing Council
and the British High Commission,' they told me. 'Doctor
Barnett, the doctor in charge of the mission hospital will
pick you up around six pm.'

My head was still very muzzy when I woke up next
morning. 'Physically I'm in Africa, but mentally I still
seem to be suspended somewhere between continents,' I
told Ruth over breakfast.

The formalities passed off smoothly. My papers were
in order. Uniformed figures smiled and welcomed me to
Kenya, and if anybody noticed that I was acting as if I had
left ninety-five percent of my brain behind me in Scotland, they were far too polite to say so.

The one thing which continued to register clearly in
the small percentage of grey matter that still seemed to be
functioning was the fact that I was hot - unpleasantly hot.
And my waist-length hair was far too long and far too
heavy. 'I can't put up with this a moment longer. Take me
to a hair-dresser,' I begged Ruth at lunch-time.

Snip, snip, snip - a swift efficient clicking of scissors
and I was shorn. A newly bobbed Katie stared back at me
from the mirror. 'Thank goodness my father can't see
this!' I thought with a pang. Dad had been so proud of my
hair.

But at least the heat didn't bother me so much after
that, and by the time Dr. Bill Barnett and his wife Laura

arrived to collect me that evening, it was dark, gloriously cool and I was feeling much more like myself.

Dr. Bill shook me by the hand. He was an American in his late-forties, and, I sensed instantly, a man of outstanding dedication and strength of character. I already knew from Nettie's letters how busy the hospital was and how much responsibility rested upon him.

'We are thankful to God for sending you to help us, Katie,' he said.

'And I am thankful to be here,' I replied warmly.

Soon we had left the city behind and I began to understand why missionaries so often requested prayer for God's protection when travelling. The dirt road before us was hazardous. According to Dr. Bill there was a drop of several hundred feet on one side for part of the way, and he kept having to swerve to avoid pot-holes. At least, I consoled myself after a particularly vicious series of jolts, there's no chance of him falling asleep at the wheel!

It took us two hours to cover the thirty-five miles between Nairobi and Kijabe, but eventually, to my great relief, we reached the Mission compound.

'I suppose you have heard quite a bit about the place?' Dr. Bill remarked.

I had. I already knew that Kijabe Mission station was one of the oldest and best established mission stations in Kenya; that it was situated approximately 7,200 feet above sea-level, was surrounded by a forest of cedar and wild olive trees and overlooked the great rift valley. From the health point of view I knew that it was a good place to be working in, since the high altitude meant that there was very little malaria. I also knew that the station almost constituted a village in itself, with a radio studio, a printing press, a Bible School and three boarding-schools, as well as the hospital, all contained within the massive compound.

The darkness was frustrating. I could see next to nothing.

'Never mind. You'll be given a guided tour of the compound in the morning,' Laura assured me.

The car pulled up outside a solid-looking stone house. As we got out, the front door opened and Sylvia appeared on the door-step.

'There you are at last! Come in! Come in!' she called. 'Welcome to Kijabe, Katie. Nettie has told me so much about you.'

I was ushered into a comfortable living-room to chat, briefly over a hot bed-time drink, about the challenge of medical work in a developing country, and the privilege of serving the Lord. Then we prayed together thanking God for all His goodness to us, and remembering Nettie, who had just gone home on furlough!

It was time for bed. As I closed the door of my room behind me snippets of conversation flitted through my mind. I remembered what Nettie had told me about life on the wards, what Tom Lloyd had said about the evangelistic aims of the Mission, what everybody had seemed to say about the importance of language-learning and of identifying with African culture. I climbed into bed, and lay awake visualizing myself as a missionary-nurse. I imagined myself getting to know African people, building friendships when I was off-duty and sharing my faith as I carried out my work. There was no doubt about it, the whole thing would be a tremendous challenge. But, with God's help, I was ready and willing to take it on.

Early next morning, drawn by a shaft of sunlight

beckoning across the cement floor of my room, I slipped out onto the veranda. I could see the full length of the valley. Miles and miles of beautiful Kenyan countryside spread before me, green and fertile after the April rains. There was even a herd of giraffe, moving amongst the acacia trees on incredibly delicate legs, stretching their graceful necks to feed from the uppermost branches. As I savoured the magical calm and freshness of it all, I felt a thrill of amazement that God, the Creator of such perfection, should have His hand on my life. All I wanted, at that moment, was to justify the confidence so many people had placed in me and to glorify Him.

'How would you feel about working for a few hours this morning?' Sylvia asked me after breakfast.

'That sounds like a good idea,' I said, eager to discover for myself what nursing in a hospital in Kenya was really like.

CHAPTER FIVE

EARNING AND LEARNING

'How are you settling in, Katie? I mean, are you happy here?' Dr. Bill asked me as we snatched a cup of coffee after a pre-natal clinic.

It was now three months since my arrival in Kijabe and in many ways it seemed much longer. The work was so demanding I could hardly remember what spare time felt like. As for being happy - well - 'I've been too busy to think about it much,' I hedged.

Dr. Bill was not letting me away with that. He was not a man to make superficial inquiries, and he did not believe in superficial answers.

'Think about it now,' he prompted.

'Well, I love my work in maternity. I mean the babies are utterly adorable. It's just ...'

'Go on ...'

'It's just that I feel I'm failing as a missionary. I came here expecting to tell people about the Lord Jesus, but I can't even talk to them about ordinary everyday things.'

There I'd said it. For the first time I had given voice to the vague feelings of failure and frustration which were building up inside me.

Dr. Bill obviously understood.

'Sometimes I feel that way myself,' he said. ' But there are other ways of witnessing, Katie, and in any case, we need to earn the right to speak ...' He broke off, glancing at his watch and draining his cup. 'I'll have to go now. We will talk about this later. O.K.?'

'O.K.' I agreed, though actually I felt I had said enough. I had only just begun to face up to my own unhappiness. I needed time to think about it and to analyse it more fully before talking again.

What had gone wrong? Certainly the last three months had been the most hectic of my whole life until now. I had been working on average twelve to fifteen hours a day with night duties two nights out of three. But that wasn't the real problem. I had known life at Kijabe would not be a rest cure. The experience for which I had not been prepared was the sense of isolation: that painful lack of meaningful contact with the African people who thronged the hospital.

It stemmed, in part, from the fact that I was communicating (or rather failing to communicate) with them in English. Of course I was supposed to be learning Swahili, but somehow I could not summon the energy to concentrate on the intricacies of grammar and vocabulary. After three months I was still stammering over the most basic greetings, and only the day before I had made a real fool of myself.

I had been helping with a pre-natal clinic.

'I cannot hear my baby praying,' a young mother-to be looked at me with worried brown eyes.

Unable to work out why she should have such high expectations of a foetus *in utero*, I was forced to consult Sylvia. With her knowledge of Ki-swahili, *she* was able to grasp the problem at once. The girl had been trying to tell me that she could not *feel* her baby *playing* (i.e. moving). In other words, she was afraid her unborn child was dead.

A simple procedure followed. Then, 'There's absolutely nothing to worry about. The baby has an excellent heart-beat,' Sylvia pronounced.

How I wished I could have reassured the patient myself without being dependent on my fellow-missionaries. I was left feeling more desperate than ever to learn Ki-swahili. In the weeks that followed, however, no matter how hard Sylvia and I tried to re-arrange my workload, there just did not seem to be time for language-study.

Language-problems aside, my busy timetable gave rise to its own frustrations. The Kenyan people, I knew, were kind-hearted and hospitable, yet with such long hours of duty, I had very little opportunity to get to know them informally; and the cultural differences in our understanding of time did not help.

On my precious day off I would invite a couple of student nurses in for a meal. 'I'm on night-call, so we will have to eat at six,' I would explain carefully. 'Do you understand?'

'Oh yes,' they would assure me cheerfully. 'As for us, we will be there at six.' And invariably they would arrive, giggling shyly, at around eight o'clock, by which time the dinner had spoilt and I was due back at the hospital for a ward round.

There was no doubt about it, in certain respects my first taste of life as a missionary-nurse had been rather disappointing, and at times I felt I was having very little meaningful contact with African people. One of the most difficult aspects of my situation, however, and the one which I felt least inclined to discuss with anyone, had nothing to do with *African* culture. It concerned my relationship with my fellow missionaries.

I had known from the beginning that I would be one of a large number of A.I.M. missionaries from various parts of the globe on Kijabe Mission station. My missionary orientation course had not prepared me for the cultural differences between *us*. We shared the same faith in the same Lord. We were all seeking to glorify Him, as we fulfilled our common calling, but we did *not* all share the same understanding as to how it should be worked out in practice.

This was brought home to me very clearly when I found myself sharing a tiny two-bedroomed house, about twenty minutes walk from the hospital, with Tara, an American Missionary Nurse. Tara was a committed Christian and thought deeply about things. She was well-organised, beautifully-spoken, attractive and amusing, but initially we didn't hit it off.

Differences of view-point began to surface almost immediately. We got up one morning to find a queue of Kikuyu girls on the doorstep, all looking for work. Tara was eager to take one of them on. Since we were so busy, it would be a great blessing to have someone to keep the house clean and to prepare the vegetables for our evening meal, she argued. I interpreted things differently. 'Having household help,' I pontificated, 'is like a continuation of slave labour,' and I sent the girls packing. Tara was a short-term missionary and I was a long-termer, so I felt entitled to make the final decision.

Needless to say the disagreement did not help our relationship and over the months a net-work of tensions had developed between us. Tara loved cats and did not mind the havoc which her kitten created in our house. I *did* mind. I have always found it incredibly easy to live without a cat. At the same time I found it incredibly difficult to refrain from issuing casual invitations to all and sundry to 'come and drink tea', although I knew Tara preferred to know about visitors in advance. Add to these ingredients long working hours, no household conveniences for baking, washing or keeping house, and a considerable difference in the size of American and British missionary allowances and you do not have a recipe for household harmony.

Eventually matters came to a head.

It had been a typically hectic day in the hospital and I was on my way up to the house for something to eat. Just outside the garden gate, I bumped into a group of student nurses. They did not appear to be going anywhere in particular and it struck me that I should make the most of the opportunity.

'Look, why don't you all just come inside with me and we will drink tea together,' I suggested.

To my delight, they accepted the invitation. 'Ah, that is a good idea,' nodded the leader.

Beaming, I led the way up the path, and ushered them all into the tiny living-room. Tara was there already, relaxing in a chair by the window.

'Look, I've brought visitors!' I cried. There was a moment of icy silence. Then she sprang from her chair and disappeared into her bedroom, slamming the door so hard that the glass lamp-shade on her bedroom lamp shattered into a thousand pieces.

Outwardly, for the sake of my guests, I managed to contain myself. Inwardly, I was livid. Of course I knew my habit of casually inviting folk for tea grated on Tara. But really, this was the limit!

'What sort of a way was that to behave?' I raged when the girls had gone merrily about their way. 'I'll have you know I have every right to invite people to this house when I want to.'

'And I have every right to my privacy when I want it,' Tara replied.

We had reached the point of no return. In the row which followed all the tensions of the past months came flooding out into the open. Tara found me impossible to live with, and I felt exactly the same about her. Later, when we had both cooled down, we were able to discuss the matter more rationally; it was not really anyone's fault, we decided, our temperaments were just too dissimilar for us to live together happily under one roof. The only sensible solution seemed to be to part company.

Dr. Bill, however, viewed the situation in a very different light when we went to him and explained that the only way we could continue to live on the same planet was in separate houses. His God was so much bigger than ours.

'No girls,' he said. 'Don't give up. Try again, and this time let God be head of your home *and* your relationship.'

If the rebuke had come from anyone else, we would probably have resented it. Coming from Dr. Bill, we took it to heart. His life was a walking testimony. He consistently went the second mile and the third mile and the fourth mile, was constantly on call, worked long hours without any of the benefits of modern equipment, and never complained. If anyone had ever earned the right to speak, he had.

Back we went with plastic smiles nailed in place and a grim determination to try out what the man had said. The fact that his theory was backed by Scripture gave his words unarguable clout!

Bleakly we faced each other across the living-room table. Humanly-speaking we would not have chosen to share a taxi, let alone a home. Apart from anything else, we were both under such pressure at work, that the prospect of making further efforts to adapt to one another seemed like the last straw.

'It's like this, Tara,' I said eventually. 'There is no way I'm going to be able to change myself to suit you, and there is no way you're going to change yourself to suit me, so all we can do is agree that from now on we will pray together every single day, no matter how mad we are with each other, and just see if God can sort something out.'

'That's O.K. by me,' Tara nodded.

Before going to bed that night, for the first time we sat down and prayed that God would fill our hearts with love for Himself and teach us how to live together to His glory. It was a step of blind obedience in accordance with what, thanks to Dr. Bill, we now perceived as being His will. We still did not have any enthusiasm for the idea. Indeed, at the back of our minds, I think we both suspected we were asking the impossible, but, theoretically, we knew we were doing the right thing.

Day after day, in the weeks which followed, we repeated that request. At first there did not seem to be much sign of an answer. We got on each others nerves as much as ever. However, at least now the whole thing was out in the open, we were able to discuss the way we felt, and gradually I began to spot a few holes in my behaviour. In the first place I realized that I had to respect Tara's right to privacy. She needed it, just as much as I needed company, in order to relax. I became less indiscriminate with my invitations, trying as far as possible to consult

Tara first. And when I forgot, and got carried away on a
wave of hospitality, creating yet another 'but what are
two chops amongst so many?' crisis, I noticed that Tara
was much more forgiving.

Several weeks after beginning to pray another area of
dissension between us was unexpectedly resolved.

Pastor Joseph, the pastor of the local A.I.C church
appeared on our door-step. I was surprised to see him. I
knew that he was a very busy man, with many responsibilities. I was even more surprised when, after a lengthy
exchange of greetings and several cups of tea, he informed me that he had come to speak to me about a matter
of some importance.

'I hear that you do not have any girl working for you,'
he said, setting his tea-cup to one side and getting down
to business.

'That is correct,' I replied with a flutter of spiritual
pride. 'In my opinion missionaries should do their own
house-work. It is all wrong for us to have African
servants.'

At this he eyed me quizzically, then proceeded to
scupper my interpretation of the matter, pointing out that
I was actually giving the community the impression that
I did not trust them.

I was shocked. 'Really and truly the only reason I said
we didn't want help was because it didn't seem right.
Please, you must believe me. The thought of the girls
being dishonest never crossed my mind.'

The upshot of the thing was that a few days later Beth
came into our lives. She was a young mother in difficult
circumstances, and, from her point of view, the job was
a godsend. And the blessing was by no means one way.
It was more restful, I realized, to live in a house where you

did not always have to run a plough from the door to wherever you wanted to go. In fact, Beth's help made our home-life so much more agreeable that Tara would have been perfectly justified in shouting 'I told you so' from the roof-top. But the words never crossed her lips - not even in a whisper. The prayer-times which had started off simply to enable us to share the same home, had by this stage become times of praise and thanksgiving to God and of intercession for others. It was further proof, if we had needed it, that God really was at work in our relationship.

Unbelievably I had been in Kenya for over six months and the time had come to write my very first Christmas prayer letter. I chewed the end of my pencil, scribbled a few sentences, scored them out and started again. How very difficult it was to know what to say. Eventually I got something on paper:

Dear Folks,

Merry Christmas to you all and a very Happy New Year when that comes round.

Home and all that it holds dear, is very much in my mind and heart just now as I think about Christmas. I would love to be able to see the snow on the hills of Bonnie Scotland as we celebrate the Saviour's birth, but He is as precious to me here in Kenya as He was at home ...

Tara and I share a house here. We have grown one or two wisdom teeth since we came together which enable us now to enjoy our home.

Do please pray specially for single girls who

serve the Lord abroad. Married women can choose their housemates but we cannot, and it is so important to have love and harmony in a home ...

How many people would read between the lines, I wondered? Jean would, but then, she knew the inside story, and all along her letters had provided me with a life-line of loving advice. She knew my faults and my struggles, and yet she never made me feel that I was failing as a missionary. But would my many other prayer partners be so understanding? How would they react if I were to be absolutely blunt and say that a major achievement in my first seven months in Kenya, had been to learn to love and respect a missionary colleague?

And yet it had been a lesson of such vital importance. Bringing and keeping relationships before the Lord, I was learning, is as necessary on the Mission field as it is at home. Perhaps even more so, because people are more vulnerable to real and imagined slights outside their own culture. My relationship with Tara could so easily have been a spiritual stumbling-block, but instead God had shown us how to make it work to His glory.

This experience gave me confidence to believe that He would also help me to work to His glory as a missionary-nurse. It was still a little disappointing to look back over the past seven months and see areas in which I had made so little progress. Language-study was an on-going problem. I had not had any opportunities to share the gospel. I still felt as if I wasn't really coming to grips with African culture. However I was now prepared to abandon my preconceived ideas of what I ought to achieve. 'I have learned in whatsoever state I am, therewith to be content,' Paul had written from the frustrations and limitations of his prison cell. His words were a challenge to me. Yes, I finally decided, as I put the finishing touches to my prayer letter, despite a certain degree of frustration at my own limitations, I, too, could say I was content.

CHAPTER SIX

LITEIN

'Katie, wait a minute. I would like a word with you.'

I was about to dash home for lunch when Dr. Bill called me aside. Life at Kijabe hospital had just returned to normal after our New Year festivities and we were as busy as ever. What could he want? I noticed the type-written envelope in his hand. To judge from his expression it was not good news.

'This may come as rather a shock,' he continued in a serious manner. 'The fact is we received word this morning that the Nairobi Office want to alter your assignment. The nurse who runs Litein Dispensary is about to return to the States on sick-leave and they want you to cover for her.'

'What! Leave Kijabe!' I gasped.

'Well, only for three months.'

Momentarily I was speechless. Then questions flooded into my mind.

Dr. Bill answered as best he could. I was being asked to go to Litein because the place needed a qualified nurse-midwife, he explained. It was a very different situation to Kijabe, away out in the bush, on the other side of the Mau Forest. By the end of our interview I was simply *itching* to know more.

'I haven't been able to concentrate on anything since I heard the news,' I said to Tara that evening. 'What do you suppose it will be like?'

'I'll tell you what,' said Tara. 'We'll get a day off together next week and spy out the land.'

And so, the following Wednesday morning we left Kijabe to drive eighty miles eastwards to Kericho and then on to Litein.

Before coming out to Kenya, I had heard the country described as a land of infinite variety and now I had the opportunity to see some of this variety for myself. In under two hours we had exchanged the steep escarpments of the Kijabe region for the undulating hills and tea plantations of the area around Kericho. The tea-pickers fascinated me. They were out in their hundreds in their wide-brimmed cone-shaped hats and rubber aprons, plucking the leaves from the top of the tea-bushes at tremendous speed and tossing them into the baskets on their backs. I refrained from taking photographs, though, knowing that some tribes believed this was equivalent to stealing the subject's soul. The last thing I wanted to do was to introduce a note of discord to that colourful scene.

At Kericho we stopped and had afternoon tea in the Tea Hotel. More variety! I couldn't get over the *Englishness* of the place. Sitting there in the shade, sipping tea and disposing of wafer-thin sandwiches, it was as if we had been transported back in time, to another era, not to mention another world. The variety and colours of the flowering bushes in the garden took my breath away.

But it was goodbye to gentility from then on; the thirty-five mile drive from Nairobi to Kijabe had been a Sunday school outing compared with that twenty-two mile haul from Kericho to Litein. At least between Nairobi and Kijabe there was a road. Between Kericho and Litein there was nothing but a dirt track; twenty-two miles of soft black cotton-seed soil which clung to everything. We saw a number of cars abandoned here and there along a particularly muddy stretch, and hoped with all our hearts that we would not be forced to do the same thing ourselves. By the time we reached our destination, we both looked as if we had just come from a ploughing match, and we both realized that our return journey could be difficult. With the rainy season just tailing off, there was every possibility of an afternoon downpour.

'If that mud becomes slippier, we will never be able to drive through it,' Tara observed.

It seemed preferable to avoid getting caught in a cloud-burst. Sally Allen, the nurse whose place I was due to be taking, welcomed us very warmly. We ate delicious pineapple, drank tea, and after a brief chat and a quick tour of the Dispensary, hopped back into the car and set off for home. To our relief, we reached the tarmac road in Kericho without experiencing anything more alarming than the odd slither.

We had plenty to discuss. Tara had found the whole set-up pretty depressing: in her eyes the Dispensary, with its slanted tin roof and high chain-link fence, resembled a fortified hen-house. 'Poor Katie, imagine being cooped up in a place like that!' she sympathized.

I was a little more positive. My brief chat with Sally had been enough to show me that despite its ramshackle appearance,* Litein dispensary was a very busy place, and the challenge appealed to my adventurous spirit. There was only one cloud on the horizon as far as I was concerned. Sally had mentioned that she did a great deal

*Thanks to the generosity of the Christoffelblinden Mission, Litein Dispensary has since been extended and renovated.

of dental work, and my adventurous spirit was not quite
equal to that.

'Still, I'm looking forward to it. Everyone seemed so
friendly,' I recalled.

'And it *is* only for three months,' Tara added.

Despite my sadness at parting from Tara, the very moment I moved to Litein a sense of excitement gripped me.

'What a lot of space for one missionary!' I kept
thinking as I settled in. This was partly due to the fact that
I had moved into a mission house with three bedrooms
instead of the usual two. But gradually I realized that I
had a greater sense of cultural space as well. Kijabe
Mission Station, by the very nature of its scope and size,
and the large number of Westerners who worked there,
had prevented me from coming into contact with the
realities of tribal life. Even the Kenyan people there
spoke with an American accent and had a western value
system.

Now, at last, I was living and working almost solely
with African people. I could count my missionary colleagues on the fingers of one hand; there was Dr. Ellen
Norton, her husband - Dick, and Ruth Mitchell, an
Australian nurse, who (bless her!) had relieved me of all
responsibility for the Dispensary books. Everyone else
for miles around was Kipsigis.

I quickly came to the conclusion that the Kipsigis
people, with their gentle manners, fine features and
delicate build, were one of the friendliest and most
attractive peoples of the world. I loved their sense of
humour, which seemed so similar to my own. Day by day
they streamed to the Dispensary, waiting patiently for

attention, always smiling, always polite. I had never done a course in child care, but suddenly I discovered that when a Kipsigis child was sick, the parents would sooner bring it to me for attention than go anywhere else. When I tried to explain, as I sometimes had to, that the child's illness required treatment in the government hospital, they would reluctantly agree to take the child there - but they were happiest when I could treat the child myself. I was amazed and touched by what seemed an almost intuitive recognition of my love for wee people.

At the same time, I could not help wishing that there would be a similar recognition of the fact that I loathed dentistry. Sally, apparently, had extracted patients' teeth on a regular basis without turning a hair and the same was expected of me. Within a few days of my arrival, a Kipsigis woman had appeared at the clinic with her little boy, holding her jaw, and telling me through a dramatic series of grimaces and gestures that her problem was toothache. What was I going to do about it?

Steeling myself, I escorted her out of the Dispensary and sat her on a chair in the sun. Almost immediately a crowd of spectators gathered round. I brought Sally's dental instruments, and arming myself with the one that resembled a pair of pliers, got down to business. Three excruciating minutes later my frantic yanking bore fruit. To the great delight of the spectators, out into the tropical sunlight came a huge rotten back molar. The woman uttered a grunt of satisfaction; then, reflectively, pursed her lips and spat a ball of blood into the bushes. For my part, I bolted across to my house in order to recover from the procedure over a soothing cup of coffee.

It was some minutes before I returned to the scene. My patient greeted me with gratitude tinged with querulousness. Where on earth had I got to, she seemed to ask? And then, to my horror, I noticed her little boy seated in the dental chair at the centre of an expectant crowd - open-mouthed.

'Oh no!' I groaned inwardly. 'Not another one!'

This extraction, however, proved to be much easier. Still, in the weeks that followed, I was never able to handle dental-work with anything touching Sally's matter-of-fact competence. For me, it was always a nightmare.

I adapted to the other aspects of the work more easily. My new responsibilities - diagnosing at the Dispensary, running busy wards and supervising an entirely African staff - did not weigh as heavily as I might have expected. It was the attitude of the people I was working with that made the crucial difference. The ward staff consisted of five older women and a number of teenage girls. The older women had been working in the Dispensary for years and were very experienced in diagnosing and dealing with the common medical problems. Despite the fact that I could not speak a word of Kipsigis, they were exceptionally kind and accommodating.

To begin with I simply assumed their attitude was typically Kipsigis, but as time went by and I got to know them better, I realized that there was more to it than this. Their kindness *was* partly natural, but it was also deliberate. The five women actually had a deliberate policy of being kind to missionaries.

This had its roots in the life-story of the leader of the group, a woman called Sarah Jane. Sarah Jane had been born in the early thirties at a time when it was still customary for babies born to uncircumcized mothers to be smothered at birth. According to tribal law the midwives could not permit such babies to live because an uncircumcized girl was still technically a child, and a child could not give birth to a child. Presumably Sarah Jane's mother had found herself in just such a position. In an attempt to save her baby's life, she had given birth in a field and had then hidden tiny Sarah under a hedge. There, Mrs. Anderson, the grandmother of a missionary working in Litein, had discovered her and had brought the child home and lovingly cared for her right up until the time of her death, some ten years later. Ever since, in loving memory of what Mrs. Anderson had done for her, Sarah Jane had gone out of her way to help any missionaries who came to Litein, and had encouraged the other members of staff to do the same.

As a result of her good offices, I learned more about local culture in one month in Litein than I had in six at Kijabe. It was Sarah Jane who taught me how to prepare traditional Kipsigis food and who helped me to communicate with the local people, confiding in me, as our relationship developed, some of the joys and the hurts of the past.

In part her stories tended to confirm some of the accusations which have been levelled at missionaries over the years. She told me of occasions when she had suffered as a result of Western insensitivity; times when her hospitality had been shunned or her values disregarded. Yet even though she spoke quite readily of such incidents, it was always without rancour. The missionaries had come; they had made mistakes; but at the same time they had communicated the life-transforming knowledge of a living loving Saviour. The hurts had long since been forgiven and only gratitude remained. As I got to know the Kipsigis people better, I was to discover that

this was a common attitude amongst the older genera-
tion.

Very often when we begin a new job there is a stage of
novelty when everything and everybody appears in a rosy
hue and we throw ourselves joyfully into the work. It is
easy to appreciate God's power and presence at such
times. It is not so easy when routine sets in, when
pressures, tensions and conflicts develop, when we grow
tired - and irritable...

By the end of my first few months in Litein, I had
grown very irritable indeed. Not only had busy working
days and lack of sleep taken their toll, but there was the
additional strain of constantly struggling to adapt to
another culture.

This may seem contradictory after all I have just said
about my delight in being part of an African set-up. It
isn't really. At one level I continued to cherish the
privilege of working with and of learning from my
African colleagues as much as ever; but equally I had to
admit that coping on a daily basis with the experiential
reality that their ways were not my ways was far from
easy. Values, priorities, thought-processes - all were
different! Add to this my inability to speak the language
and you have the ingredients for a great deal of frustration
and misunderstanding.

Of course in theory I had come prepared to adjust. I
understood that my Western background had taught me
to think individualistically and to be activity-orientated,
while my African friends tended to think communally
and to be relationship-orientated. Quite a lot of the time,
I genuinely felt that the African way was best. The

concept of the extended family and the emphasis on resolving disagreements regardless of how long it took, struck me as being much closer to the Christian ideal than the nuclear families and clock-watching of the West. However, in practice, when it came down to basic patient-care and I discovered that the prevailing cultural ethos leant itself to bad nursing practice, adjustment seemed out of the question.

There was an element of fatalism in the thinking of the Kenyan staff which meant that they were inclined to give up on critically-ill patients and to regard death as inevitable. This was anathema to me. I could not bear to think that a patient might suffer or even die in the Dispensary as a result of some neglect on my part or on the part of the nursing staff. Of course I could see why death was accepted so much more readily here. It was a tragically common occurrence. Yet I could not believe that the Lord Jesus, who had fed five thousand hungry people and wept over the city of Jerusalem, would wish me to concern myself less with the life of an individual patient in Litein than I would have done with his or her Western counterpart, just because the African patient was one of so many. I was aware of a very real culture gap, and did not know how to get across it.

I ended up doing a lot of shouting. It seemed the only way to ensure that patients got the standard of care they required. And some of it, I must confess, was the result of sheer frustration, bad-temper and impatience. It would have been so much better if I could have quietly explained my point of view in Kipsigis. But I was restricted to using English and so many situations called for an instant reaction - which in my case was generally a yell!

I always felt guilty about it afterwards and would pray

fervently that God would forgive me and help me to control my temper. Yet time after time outrage got the better of me.

Eventually, one afternoon, I had a visit from the chairman of the Dispensary Management Committee. He struck me as a fierce little man, the Pastor! I was decidedly in awe of him. While I ran the Dispensary from day to day, the Management Committee was responsible for the policy decisions, for the hiring and firing of staff and matters of general discipline. And if they decided that I was not the right person for Litein dispensary, they could ask the Mission to send me elsewhere.

As soon as I opened the door I realized that this was not a social call. The Pastor was upset. In fact he was so upset that he had brought Peter, the local Mission representative, along with him to act as interpreter.

For well over half an hour, via Peter, he laid down the law. Who did I think I was to go round shouting at the nurses? That was not the way to conduct myself in African society. Africans believed in politeness not shouting. My behaviour was offensive, and what's more, it was unchristian. Did not the Scriptures clearly teach that Christians should keep control of their tongues?

Every word he spoke shot home with the stinging truth of a well-aimed arrow. I could deny nothing, nor was there anything I could say to justify myself. I could not even promise, with any degree of assurance, that the shouting would come to an end. I had already prayed so hard and so often about the problem ... and then a strange thing happened. For no apparent reason the Pastor suddenly stopped scolding. Like sunshine after a thunderstorm, his fierce glare became a fatherly smile and he stretched out his hand towards me, addressing me gently.

I looked at Peter questioningly.

'Well here's one for the record!' Peter was obviously as taken aback as I was at the change of tone. 'He says the Kipsigis people can forgive you in spite of everything, because you love their children.'

Perhaps it was my imagination, but it really seemed as if more children than ever were brought to the Dispensary after that. I would not have minded if they had come in their hundreds and kept me working twenty-four hours a day. The Pastor's words had restored my spiritual vision. I saw that despite my faults, the Kipsigis people had not written me off. Neither had God. The tiredness, the language-problems, the cultural adjustments faded into insignificance before a renewed certainty that in Litein I was indeed at the centre of His will.

Sally was due to return at the end of June and as May drew to a close I had to prepare myself for the move back to Kijabe. It was extremely painful. The thought of leaving the Kipsigis people now filled me with dismay. I prayed earnestly that God would help me to be positive about it, reminding myself how nice it would be to see Tara again. Nettie had returned from furlough. Another plus. As the days went by, however, all that happened was that my sense of belonging in Litein grew stronger than ever.

Finally it struck me that perhaps this desire ought not to be resisted; that perhaps, through it, God was trying to tell me something.

'Father, is it Your will for me to stay here?' I asked, scarcely daring to trust, but unable to deny the deep sense of peace that came upon me as I spoke.

Less than a week later that peace was confirmed. A letter arrived from A.I.M. Headquarters. I have kept it to this very day.

Dear Katie,

Greetings from the office here in Nairobi. Sally's medical report has arrived and it appears that her problems could be due to an allergy caused by the plants growing in the Litein area. She will therefore be unable to return. It seems to us as though you have found your niche there, so we would be happy if you would consider Litein Dispensary as your permanent assignment...

CHAPTER SEVEN

THE CULTURE GAP

Settling permanently into Litein was an experience in itself. Sally returned to pack up her belongings and have them transported to her new Mission home in a desert area. No danger of plant life causing asthma there! A fellow missionary slithered up the muddy road to the house with my belongings tied to the back of his pick-up.

'You know, Katie, the seat you brought has a bed hidden in it that would sleep four big people!' one of my helpers marvelled at the sight of my divan.

Four big people to a double-bed. Expectations were so different here! The single beds in the Dispensary were frequently occupied by two patients, both sick and both requiring good nursing care. And, as I had already discovered, my expectations of what that nursing care should entail were not necessarily those of the national staff.

Christmas 1973 saw me celebrating my permanent assignment with a full-scale garden party. All my African friends and their relatives and their relatives' friends piled into my small garden in the blistering afternoon heat. We sang carols and ran a three-legged race around the avocado tree, feasting on bread and jam sandwiches, washed down with gallons of Coca Cola. At the height of the festivities I produced a sisal rope. Although none of my guests had ever heard of a tug-of-war before, they

quickly grasped the principle, and soon a team of Kipsigis
men were pitting their strength against a team of Kipsigis
women. The women won - effortlessly. Working in the
fields all day had made them the stronger sex!

Yet despite the fun and laughter, and my very great
delight in staying on in Litein, I was soon to become more
aware than ever of the culture gap.

A few days after the party, a tiny premature girl,
weighing only two and a half pounds was brought into the
Dispensary. Her name was Chepkirui. She had been born
in the Mau forest and her mother had died giving birth.
Immediately I began to feed the child a carefully meas-
ured quantity of milk, praying that she would be able to
keep it down. Then, painstakingly, I explained to the
nurses on duty exactly how much and how often Chepkirui
was to be fed. I left the ward to hold a clinic. I returned
some hours later only to find they had completely neglected her.

'This is inexcusable!' I raged. 'Did I not tell you how
important it was that this little one should have milk?'

'Yes, Katie,' the girls chorused.

'Did you not tell me you understood perfectly everything I was saying?'

'Yes, Katie. As for me, I understood,' they assured
me, one after another.

'Then why did you not do as I said?' I shrieked.

The girls hung their heads and were silent. 'Katie,'
one of them muttered eventually. 'We have made you
angry. We are very sorry.'

At this point it began to dawn on me that there might
be something more than laxness behind their behaviour.
I remembered Sarah Jane's history, and the Kipsigis
attitude to babies born to uncircumcized mothers. What

was the local attitude to premature babies? I made some inquiries. It turned out to be as I suspected: my instructions about Chepkirui had foundered on the reef of fatalism. The Kipsigis people did not believe that premature babies were meant to live, for surely if God had intended them to live, He would have caused them to be born full-term. In vain I tried to impress upon the nursing staff that this was not the case; that God wanted Chepkirui to live; that He had sent His Son to die for her and had given us the responsibility of caring for her. The reef was impenetrable. As long as I was on the ward the girls would feed and tend Chepkirui, but as soon as my back was turned they ignored her. I resorted to threats.

'Any nurse who neglects Chepkirui, or any other patient for that matter, will be fired on the spot. Is that clear?'

'Yes, Katie,' the girls responded, but I knew the problem of caring for small sick babies was far from solved.

In fact it became more complex. A few weeks later another baby, a little boy this time, was brought to the Dispensary. He was called Kipngeno. His mother had given birth normally in the World Gospel Mission Hospital twenty-six miles away, then died shortly afterwards. Kipngeno had failed to thrive. Now, at the age of three months, he weighed only five pounds and was exhibiting a very strange set of symptoms. He would feed hungrily and appear satisfied; then suddenly his mouth would twist to an impossible angle up the side of his face, his eyes would become huge and staring, and he would vomit up the entire contents of his stomach. Often, after such an attack, he would run a high fever. I had never come across a case like it. By the end of his first week in the dispensary he had lost another pound.

Very quickly I noticed that the girls paid even less attention to Kipngeno than they did to Chepkirui. This time, when I took them to task, their response was devastatingly direct.

'That baby was cursed by the witch-doctors,' they informed me. 'There is no point in looking after him. He is going to die.'

'What nonsense!' I spluttered. But Kipngeno's symptoms were so strange, and the girls seemed so sure of themselves that I decided to investigate. The next day I drove the twenty-six miles to consult the doctor who had been present at Kipngeno's birth. Rather sheepishly I told him what the girls had said.

'How long have you been in Kenya?' he inquired.

'About eighteen months,' I replied.

'And you've never come across anything like this before?'

'No, of course not.' I was growing impatient now. I had expected him to knock the supernatural theory firmly on the head and recommend some practical treatment I could give Kipngeno.

'That's why I'm here. I was hoping you could tell me what was wrong with the child.'

'All I can tell you is that there was absolutely no pathological reason for the boy's mother to die, and in medical terms there doesn't seem to be any explanation for his present condition. Over the years I've been forced to take this cursing business seriously. I've seen the pattern again and again ... curses followed by inexplicable deaths ... our Western minds find it hard to accept, but out here, quite simply, it's a fact of life.'

My mind was still reeling as I drove back to Litein. Of

course my reading of Scripture had taught me to believe in the existence of an evil power actively opposed to the rule of God upon earth. In fact I had noticed in my own Christian experience that often when I took a step of faith in obedience to God I would encounter inexplicable obstacles and difficulties. Satan was indeed alive and active in the world, I believed. But never before had I encountered a manifestation of evil such as this: a tiny child dying as the result of a curse! I felt sick at the thought.

As soon as I got back I asked the three other Litein missionaries to come round to my house.

'You look worried, Katie,' Dick observed as I passed round cups of coffee. 'What's the problem?'

I explained about Kipngeno. 'It really looks as if the cause of his illness is demonic,' I concluded. 'I have tried all the conventional treatments and they aren't working.'

In the pause that followed, I could see my own feelings of inadequacy reflected on the faces of my three colleagues. We were out of our depth. Nothing in our medical training had prepared us to combat the effects of a witch-doctor's curse. Our Bible College training, however, had taught us to seek God's guidance in Scripture. And so we turned to Luke's Gospel, to the passage where Jesus heals a demon-possessed man. We read the incident aloud and then discussed its implications.

We were all struck by the way in which the demons cowered before Jesus.

'As God's Son, Jesus had complete authority over every spiritual power,' Dick observed. 'I reckon that authority is as real today as it was two thousand years ago. His power is far greater than the power of any witch-doctor.'

Suddenly the way forward seemed very clear. Together in the name of Jesus we prayed that God would heal Kipngeno, just as He had healed that demon-possessed man. We asked Him to break the hold of evil upon that little boy's life, to guard and protect his future. It was simple. It was unspectacular. But the sense of Christ's presence was real. The heaviness of spirit which I had known since my conversation with the doctor left me, and in its place came a sense of expectation.

I fed Kipngeno as usual that evening at ten o'clock. When he had taken his fill I cradled his tiny emaciated body in my arms ... watching ... praying ... The minutes ticked past. Eventually, scarcely able to grasp the miracle that had taken place, I laid him back in his cot - sound asleep. He had not vomited. His face had remained normal. 'Thank you, oh thank you Lord,' I breathed.

'God has healed Kipngeno. He's keeping his food down!' I was just bursting to pass the news on to the nurses next morning. But even though all Kipngeno's unnatural symptoms - the twisted mouth, glazed eyes, sudden fevers - had evidently disappeared, the girls were unimpressed. What could I, an *mzungu* (or European) know of the power of curses? No baby who had been cursed had ever recovered in their experience. To my great disappointment and intense irritation I saw that they still wanted to have as little to do with Kipngeno as before.

That afternoon I returned from my lunch-break to find one of the nurses, a happy-go-lucky teenager, lounging against a wall, completely oblivious to the fact that a critically ill child was in need of something to drink. My confidence in my ability to communicate things to the nursing staff hit rock bottom. Nothing I said or did seemed to have the slightest impact. 'You are fired,' I told the girl sharply. 'Just pack your box and go.'

Afterwards I regretted my words. I did not regret the decision, for the girl would never have made a nurse - her attitude had always been flippant - but I should at least have had the grace to explain this to her. Then there was the Dispensary Management Committee to consider. Hiring and firing of staff was their prerogative, not mine. There would be recriminations ... the Pastor would fume ... oh dear! Forcibly I dismissed one unpleasant prospect from my thoughts only to find another problem rearing its head. From Monday I was officially on holiday. But how could I look forward to the break after what had happened? What was to become of Kipngeno and Chepkirui in my absence? How could I possibly abandon them for a fortnight?

The answer, when I hit upon it, seemed so obvious I was amazed it hadn't occurred to me sooner. I would take Kipngeno and Chepkirui on holiday with me. It was not as if I had been planning to go very far. All I wanted was an escape from the Dispensary routine - two weeks of peace and quiet, reading, eating and sleeping under my own roof. I had always had the feeling that my house was far to large for a single missionary. Obviously it had been designed to accommodate cots in the spare room!

The following day cots, baby clothes, feeding equipment and babies were taken out of the ward and installed in my home. The Dispensary staff, by this stage, had become so used to my brain-storms that they simply rolled their eyes to heaven and said nothing. My missionary colleagues were more vocal. 'You *are* supposed to be having a *holiday*,' I was reminded. But though getting up at two a.m. and again at four a.m. to feed and change

babies might not have been anyone else's idea of a
holiday, it suited me down to the ground. I revelled in the
opportunity to care for Kipngeno and Chepkirui twenty-
four hours a day without interruption. At last I had time
not only to wash them and feed them, but to play with
them, to cuddle them, to pray over them. And how they
thrived on the extra attention! By the end of that fortnight
I felt totally refreshed, and my two sick babies were well
on the road to gurgling good health.

The night before I was due to go back on duty I stood
at the foot of their cots watching them as they slept. Their
cheeks had filled out I noted with pride. Then came the
inevitable pang at the thought of parting from them. Of
course I would see them every day at the Dispensary, but
that was not the same. They were still so weak. Back at
the Dispensary they could so easily lose ground. 'I would
be the most foolish nurse in Kenya if I let that happen,'
I concluded, turning out the light and climbing beneath
my mosquito net. 'I will keep them here for another two
weeks.'

Two *months* later Kipngeno and Chepkirui were still
with me - pounds heavier, bright-eyed and full of mis-
chief. During the day a nurse from the Dispensary would
keep an eye on them. At night the responsibility was all
mine ... ten o'clock feeds ... two o'clock feeds ... six
o'clock feeds. If anyone inquired how we were getting
on, I told them the arrangement suited me fine. This was
an understatement. I was actually experiencing the most
profound sense of fulfilment imaginable. The experience
went far beyond sentiment; sentiment wears thin at two
in the morning when faced with yet another dirty nappy
and the prospect of a day's work ahead. My joy in caring
for Kipngeno and Chepkirui had deeper roots; spiritual

roots which seemed to draw strength from God, giving me fresh insight into His love.

In the past I had sometimes been asked how an omnipotent all-loving heavenly Father could permit innocent children to starve to death. I had pointed out in reply, that God was all-powerful and all-loving, but that He had given us free will, and so, when children died as a result of our selfish mismanagement of the world's resources, it was our fault, not God's. Now, as I cared for Kipngeno and Chepkirui my former theorizing took on a new force and immediacy. A verse from Matthew's Gospel kept running through my mind: 'Inasmuch as you have done it unto one of the least of these my brethren, you have done it unto me.' The amazing truth that God loved these two little ones so much that He actually identified with them broke freshly upon me, filling me with joy; and with the joy came a growing conviction that this was the work He had prepared for me to do - the reason I had come to Kenya. Every morning as I woke up to see those two little black faces wreathed in smiles, I felt a glowing inner assurance that the sight was even more precious to God, the brother of the least...

The question was how could I possibly hope to convey this to the nurses? Western society could *afford* to fight for the life of every child. But I was living in a country where an outbreak of measles could wipe out hundreds of previously healthy children. How could I expect nurses brought up against such a background to understand why I was making such a fuss about one premature baby? I had explained till I was blue in the face that it was never God's will for them or for anyone else to give up on small sick children; that what they needed was regular nursing care; that Kipngeno and Chepkirui were living proof of God's willingness to heal. And my words had failed to communicate.

Such was the cultural impasse that, as the days went by, I became increasingly confused. Had the Dispensary staff got it right after all, I wondered? Was it better to remain detached and to let things take their course? Should I continue to argue, or should I resign myself to their viewpoint?

The inner conflict drove me to my knees.

'Lord, please help me. Please show me what to do about this,' I prayed.

CHAPTER EIGHT

MONKEYS, MALARIA AND A MESSAGE

'I am here to tell you to come back to the Dispensary.' Nurse Hannah bounded into my living-room with the virtuous air of one who has gone well beyond the call of duty.

She could not have picked a worse moment. I had just emerged from washing my hair, which was a tangled dripping mess. 'Oh no!' I groaned inwardly. 'I never seem to have a minute's peace these days!' Resignedly I wrapped a towel around my head. 'What's the problem?' I asked.

At this the girl regarded me more virtuously than ever (clearly whatever crisis had arisen at the Dispensary, she could not be held responsible). 'There is a woman in the ward with a small small baby.'

A premature baby! I was on my feet in an instant and out through the door.

Yes, the Dispensary staff confirmed, a young Kipsigis woman *had* been brought to the Dispensary early that morning, but now she was preparing to leave. I had only just arrived in time. Breathless, I reached the Maternity Ward to find her sitting on a bed, a baby-shaped bundle by her side.

'*Chamage,*' I greeted her. 'I have come to see your baby.'

'*Achamage,*' she responded without enthusiasm and

without making any effort to show me the child. I tried again.

'I have heard your baby is very small and in need of special care.'

'You are wrong. It is not a baby. It is a monkey.'

A monkey! My jaw dropped. For the millionth time I wished I had a better grasp of the Kipsigis language. 'Let me see?' I pulled back the cloth around the mysterious bundle to reveal the puckered face of - yes, definitely - a tiny baby.

'It is a monkey,' the woman repeated woodenly, staring straight ahead.

The repetition jogged my memory. I was almost sure I had overheard the nurses using the same term ... in relation to Chepkirui. Could it be that premature babies were locally known as monkeys? Here was a woman distancing herself emotionally from her child, protecting herself from the pain of its inevitable death. A monkey, not a baby. If she could convince herself of that it would not hurt so much. Nobody felt under any moral obligation to care for a monkey. Nobody wept when a monkey died. Maybe the Dispensary Management Committee would not understand, but I knew what I had to do.

'Please let me look after your baby for you,' I pleaded.

'No.' The woman now picked up the bundle and clasped it firmly. 'You will only grow fond of it and it will die, and then you will be sorry.'

'You are right,' I agreed. 'I would be very sorry if your baby died, but perhaps if I look after it for a while, it will live and then we will both be glad.'

'It is a monkey,' the woman muttered, but her resistance had weakened, and a few moments later she placed the precious bundle into my outstretched hands.

I hurried back to the house, my steps light with elation, my mind buzzing with plans. I would have another cot brought over from the Dispensary. I would need more baby clothes too. 'Just wait till you meet Kipngeno and Chepkirui,' I murmured happily as I laid the bundle on the living-room settee and began to unwind layers of cloth. At the first sight of the tiny body underneath my heart sank. This little boy was more minute than Chepkirui when she had first come to the dispensary. Quite apart from anything else, I couldn't think where to put him. He would be *lost* in a cot. What I needed was something much smaller.

I was just about to start hunting, when I heard a truck pulling up outside my gate. Then came the sound of doors slamming - of raised voices. Something was being unloaded?

I reached the window in time to see a very large crate being dumped in my garden.

'That is the last thing I need!' I shot out of the house to give the truck driver a piece of my mind. 'What are you thinking about? Put that crate back on your lorry and take it away.'

The truck driver grinned disarmingly and scratched his head. 'Are you Miss Katie MacKinnon?'

I nodded.

'Then this crate's for you.'

'But I haven't ordered anything!' I glared at the crate and gradually my feelings became tinged with curiosity. Since the truck driver could not be intimidated into removing it, there was only one thing to be done.

'Let's get it open!' The words brought a dozen delighted spectators scrambling over the fence to my assistance. Joyfully they surrounded the crate, pushing and prising; then came the sound of splintering wood as one of the boards was raised. A dozen eager faces turned towards me, eyes alight with anticipation.

'I wonder what's inside?' The moment of climax. I tried to inject some enthusiasm into my voice, but all I could think of was the minute premature baby I had left on the living-room settee. James, the Dispensary lab technician (and general handy-man) obligingly prised off another piece of wood.

'It looks like a glass box.'

What! I elbowed James aside to feel for myself. Sure enough beneath the wooden boards I could see a smooth glass surface.

'Quick, quick - get it out! But *please* be careful!' My head was reeling. I could hardly believe what my senses were telling me. It was a miracle! A miracle of provision for the tiny occupant of my settee!

Inside the crate there was an incubator.

When God does something, He takes care of every detail. Many times I have known expensive pieces of equipment to be damaged in transit; but this incubator, which had travelled all the way from the United States (it had been shipped one year previously, at Sally's request) had arrived in perfect working order. It was on a stand with a plug already attached to the wire. I was able to wheel it straight into the house, fill the appropriate compartment with water and switch on the power. Everything had been timed and planned to perfection, right down to the size of the plug.

I had asked God to show me what to do, and now, just when I was least expecting it, He had gloriously given me my answer. The arrival of that incubator was a sign. A sign of His love for premature babies. A sign to me personally. Overwhelmed with thankfulness I laid Kipkoech (for that was the baby's name) beneath the glass and watched him feebly kick his legs. He would live - I was sure of that - and I would continue to do everything I could to fight the tide of infant mortality, to love and to care for small sick babies...

A tap on the window interrupted my musings, bringing me back to the present. Kipkoech's mother had summoned the courage to come over to my house to find out what exactly had been going on. When I showed her her son she was *horrified*. 'I thought you said you would care for him! But what have you done? You have taken off all his clothes and put him in a glass box, and see, already there is a tape worm coming out of his nose!'

It was not a tape-worm, I assured her, it was a stomach tube, so that I could give Kipkoech milk. Then I explained about the incubator.

'You are telling me God sent it specially!' Her eyes were huge.

'That's right, 'I nodded.

Still shaking her head in amazement, and evidently torn between the conviction that I was mad and the hope that I might be right, the woman returned to the Dispensary. Within the hour other maternity patients were arriving on my doorstep, all agog to discover what in the world she was talking about. Word spread to the village. Soon 'the baby in the glass box' was having so many visitors I asked the Dispensary Evangelist to come to my house and talk to the people. It was a wonderful opportunity for him to share the good news of the gospel and to explain the amazing way in which God had undertaken for the children. Frequently I would arrive home to find him relating Kipkoech's story to yet another group of

wide-eyed admirers, with Kipngeno and Chepkirui along-
side, cooing engagingly in their cots. Then came the red
letter day when Kipkoech's mother beckoned me aside:

'Me, I have learned something very important,' she
announced.

'And what is that?' I prompted.

'There are no monkeys.' She beamed and pointed
towards the incubator. 'There are only babies.'

Deeply moved, I put my arms around her. It was a
moment of heartfelt joy and gratitude.

In his first letter to the Corinthians Paul speaks of the
way God uses the weak things of this world to confound
the things that are mighty, and now I was experiencing
this for myself. My clumsy arguments had achieved
little, but weak little Kipkoech in his incubator was being
used to touch people's hearts. For the first time there was
recognition that with special care the smallest and most
vulnerable members of the community could have a
future, and a Kipsigis woman, in great wonder, had
expressed this in her own Kipsigis way.

One immediate consequence of this was that my
family grew. Before long two more babies, a little boy
and a little girl, were brought to me. Kipkirui had been
born prematurely and took Kipkoech's place in the
incubator. Chebet arrived suffering from bad kwashiorkor
(a condition of protein deficiency which causes a reddish
discoloration of the hair and peeling scaly skin). Her
mother had died in childbirth.

With my nursery family now numbering five, I wondered what the Church Leaders would have to say. It
turned out that they were more than happy with the new
arrangement and even suggested that the Dispensary
nurses should be rotated through my house as part of their

'well baby' training. I thought this an excellent idea.

In the post, a few days later, I had a letter from Jean. Typically, with so much going on, my side of the correspondence had been neglected. I had not written to her for some time and my last letter had been composed during one of those periods when my single state had been getting me down. (The fact that I had accepted this, did not mean that it did not hurt from time to time.) It wasn't the sort of thing I generally shared with my prayer partners, but I counted on Jean not only to pray for my work, but for my emotional needs as well.

Now she was writing to tell me about something that had happened during their family prayer time. As usual, she had been asking God to help and encourage me, when out of the blue, one of the children, a six-year-old, had chipped in, thanking God with great conviction that Auntie Katie wasn't lonely any more.

'I haven't a clue where he got the idea from,' Jean concluded. 'But I certainly hope he's right.'

'He's as right as right could be,' I wrote back. 'Since my last letter God has filled my house with babies and I have never been so happy in my life!'

Everything had happened so fast. It seemed as if one minute I had been a full-time nurse/midwife, and the next I was a working mother of five. For my part, I could only stand back and marvel at the way God had brought this about, but I knew that from the official point of view my position would require some explaining. Just because I felt called to care for five children did not necessarily mean that the Church Office in Nairobi would see it that way. I had been assigned to the Dispensary and caring for Kipngeno and Co. was bound to take up a good bit of my time. Also, there was the financial aspect: how could I hope to support five children on an allowance designed for a single missionary?

These points were put to me very forcibly by a missionary friend who appeared on my doorstep one evening, armed with a Bible.

'I'm trusting God to provide,' I told her. 'I believe He brought the children into the house so He will supply the money for food and the strength I need to do my work.'

'But mightn't you be deluding yourself?' she countered. 'Isn't it possible that you have allowed this to happen in order to meet your own emotional needs? I mean, it seems to me that if God had intended you to have children, He would have given them to you in the conventional way. Look at what the Scripture says.'

She proceeded to open the Bible at 1 Corinthians 7:34, and read the verse aloud.

There is a difference also between a wife and a virgin. The unmarried woman careth for the things of the Lord, that she may be holy both in body and in spirit: but she that is married careth for the things of the world, how she may please her husband.

I was not quite sure what bearing that particular Scripture had on my situation, but I knew what she was getting at. After all, I had always loved babies. Still, I was not prepared to accept that I had somehow engineered my present situation. As far as I was concerned it wasn't the physical and emotional bond with my five charges which gave me the greatest fulfilment, it was my perception of God's special love for them; the fact that through them, He was revealing something of His fatherly concern for those who had the least hope of survival in human terms.

That fatherly involvement became even more apparent to me in the weeks which followed. Before I had even got round to praying seriously about finances, extra money started to flow in. My basic monthly allowance had stayed the same, of course, but for the first time in my missionary career, I was regularly receiving undesignated gifts. It wasn't that I had put out an appeal for extra funds (that would have been totally contrary to A.I.M. principles), or even hinted at the need in a prayer letter (to my shame, I hadn't written one for ages), but all of a sudden people here and there were popping the odd fiver in an envelope and asking that it should be passed on to me. The sums were never large and I never had money left over from one month to the next. But this only added to the wonder of it. Each month my expenses varied according to whether or not the children had needed medicine, and each month those additional gifts flowed in, tailor-made to cover the bills.

God was providing financially. Would He also provide me with the stamina to keep going? As my friend had pointed out, it *was* exceptionally difficult to hold down two demanding jobs and do both of them properly. I was committed to the children, but I was also committed to the Dispensary. I seemed to be constantly juggling with priorities, and in the wake of my colleague's lecture, I prayed harder than ever that God would help me not to let either commitment slip.

For a few months it seemed that this prayer too was being positively answered. All the balls stayed in the air. The children thrived and the Dispensary ran smoothly. In fact I was on the point of congratulating myself for the ease with which I mastered the dual-role technique when my delicately-balanced routine came tumbling around my ears. The cause? An outbreak of measles.

In the West measles is regarded as a fairly serious childhood disease (hence the recent emphasis on vaccination), but very rarely proves fatal. In Africa it is a different story. Measles is a foreign disease to the African continent and the children have little resistance to it. They become very ill and often die. 'Count your children *after* the measles,' runs the sober African version of a well-known proverb.

That year measles hit Litein with particular virulence. Mercifully none of the little ones in my home took sick, but the children's ward in the Dispensary was full to overflowing with small, desperately ill patients. Bang went my routine! The words 'off-duty' ceased to exist. Day and night, with the rest of the nursing staff, we moved from one emergency to another. And when it was all over and the ward was back to normal, I realized that jumping around like a grasshopper with hiccups had taken its toll.

For the first time I had to literally drag myself out of bed at night to feed the children. It was as if someone had attached bricks to my arms and legs. Not only was I exhausted, I was also assailed with doubts about my effectiveness as a missionary. Before the end of the *week*, I was flat on my back with malaria, shaking with chills and struggling to feed the children between bouts of nausea and vomiting.

Doubt liberally sprinkled with self-pity all but overwhelmed me. Why had God let this happen? Why had He even brought me to Kenya in the first place? I was a hopeless missionary. I *still* could not speak the language. I *still* kept losing my temper. I *still* had not helped anyone to faith in Christ. And now I was not even able to look after the children properly.

Eventually I propped myself up on one elbow and

reached for my Bible. Perhaps it would help to read something comforting. Unable to summon the concentration to locate a suitable passage for myself, I opened the book at random with a muttered prayer that God would speak to me. Hopefully I scanned the page.

Then Pilate therefore took Jesus and scourged him. And the soldiers platted a crown of thorns and put it on his head.

I felt a sense of total let-down. Small comfort here! Surely God realized that at a time like this the very last thing I wanted to read about was the crucifixion!

'Read it!' He seemed to insist.

So I read. Before I had reached the end of the chapter, just as I had feared, I was forced to relinquish my self-pity. There was simply no room for it in the light of the agony which Jesus had endured on my behalf. And reading further to the point in the account where Mary Magdalene learns that her Lord has actually risen from the dead, another thought struck me. Mary had been so overwhelmed by sorrow that she had not even recognized Jesus when He first spoke to her in the garden. She had mistaken Him for the gardener. Could it be that I, too, was failing to recognize Him in my own situation?

'Please open my eyes, Lord, and show me where you are in this,' I prayed.

It was as if, all along, God had been watching over me in my despondency, just waiting to respond to such a request. Light burst upon me. Since the night of my conversion I had not had such a profound awareness of His life-transforming presence. Lovingly He spoke to me, reminding me of the numbers of people who came day by day to my home to see the children and of the many opportunities the Hospital Evangelist had to speak to them of spiritual things. I had my role in that witness - not a vocal role, but the role of His appointing. He then brought a sentence in the Bible passage to my attention. I had never particularly noticed it before, but now the words seemed to jump out at me from the page. Jesus's instructions to Mary: 'Go to my brethren and say unto them I ascend unto my Father and your Father.'

I saw that Mary had been simply instructed to tell the disciples; that *they* were the ones who would take the gospel to the people.

'I am dealing similarly with you,' God seemed to say. 'The children you care for are like those disciples and one day they will take My word to their own people. You are like Mary and have a specific part to play. Receive the children, care for them and tell them of My love.'

One of the main differences between the occasions I have simply imagined God spoke to me and the times when I have truly heard His voice lies in the spiritual effect of the experience. The promptings of my own imagination tend to push me towards impulsive action, whereas the authentic voice of God inspires within me a profound sense of peace.

It was God Himself who spoke to me on this occasion, of that I am sure. As I closed my Bible and lay back on my pillows, the peace I experienced was as overwhelming as my former misery. It took root in the very core of my being. I was more certain than ever that He had called me to work with children. My limitations and failures ceased to weigh upon me. I had been given a particular sphere of influence and was called to be faithful within it... which meant, amongst other things, handing over all my anxiety about my future role...

CHAPTER NINE

'THERE WAS AN OLD WOMAN'

I recovered quickly after that, resuming my routine duties at the Dispensary with a new lightness of spirit, but soon I was facing another problem. My allowance had arrived and the additional gifts had been smaller than usual. Before long I was absolutely broke. 'What's going to happen now?' I wondered as I used up the last of our millet to make porridge for the children's breakfast. I hadn't a penny to buy more. I reassured myself with the knowledge that God would not let them go hungry. There was bound to be a cheque in the morning's mail. But to my great disappointment, James returned from his trip to the village post-office with nothing but a smile.

'You're sure there wasn't a letter for me?'

'No, Katie, the box was empty,' he beamed.

Several hours slipped by (that was one of the things I really enjoyed about being so busy - time never ever dragged) and I pushed the problem to the back of my mind. The eye-clinic demanded my full attention. At one point I even found myself stifling a giggle as an old man gazed at me through a pair of empty spectacle frames and complained vehemently that his sight was as bad as ever, despite the fact that he was 'wearing the glasses every day, just as the doctor said'!

It is easy to do the same thing in the Christian life - to look at people and situations through empty spectacle frames, forgetting we need the Spirit of God to correct our vision, I thought afterwards. How then should I be viewing the current crisis in the larder? What was God showing me through it? I had finished the clinic by this stage and was about to ponder the point over a cup of tea, when Dorcas, the student nurse on duty at my home that afternoon appeared in the door-way.

'You are having visitors,' she announced, making the most of every syllable. 'Five ladies are here to visit you.'

Sure enough a group of graceful Kipsigis women dressed in khangas and gaily coloured head-scarves were waiting in my living-room. They had come from the Africa Inland Church in the nearby village of Rungut. The Lord had spoken to them during a time of prayer, they explained and had laid it on their hearts to visit me.

'We bring gifts for you and the children,' the spokes-woman told me shyly and suddenly I saw that the table behind them was piled high with food: millet, eggs, milk, pineapples...

How *wonderful* God was! Once again, at exactly the right time He had intervened. But gloriously welcome though those gifts undoubtedly were, what the women said was even more uplifting. Like corrective glass in a pair of spectacles, their words instantly extended my vision.

'The work you are doing is a very important work,' they told me. 'We are praying that God will bless it and that it will grow.' They went on to explain that until recently there had been no such thing as an orphan in their society. If a child's parents died, it had simply been absorbed into another branch of the family circle. But with the new emphasis on education, such absorption could not happen so readily. Free primary education meant that there were no longer any older girls at home to help hard-pressed mothers care for small children. Secondary education was not free, which meant that parents had so much difficulty raising school fees for their own offspring they now thought twice before assuming responsibility for anyone else's. For the first time children were dying, not just as a result of disease and malnutrition, but because no one was prepared to offer them a home.

'Through this house God is providing a way for such children,' my visitors concluded. 'In the Rungut Church we appreciate this and we want to give you support.'

Even as they spoke I began to see my calling as potentially part of something bigger and more permanent than I had previously suspected. Evidently God had not been speaking to me in isolation, but had been laying the needs of children on the hearts of others also. Could it be that this was indeed His time to open a way for these little ones? Could it be that, as the women were praying, the work in my home would expand and grow and many more lives might be saved? With all my heart I hoped that it might be so. At the same time I knew that only God Himself could bring such a vision to pass... for from the human point of view I could see nothing but obstacles...

'Katie, Chief arap Sang is wanting to speak to you.'

It was Sarah Jane who brought me the message a few days later, beaming as usual, and completely oblivious to the fact that her words had reduced me to jelly.

'What about?' I asked.

'He didn't say. He only told me that he wanted to speak to you very soon.'

Chief arap Sang was a very important person in the local community. He was a government official with the responsibility for settling local affairs, but more than that, he was accorded all the respect which people associate with the tribal chiefs of the past.

I cast around in my mind wondering why the Chief should send for me, and concluded that I must have transgressed cultural law to the pitch where I was about to be deported.

'He is a very nice man, Chief arap Sang,' Sarah Jane tried to reassure me, but I wasn't having any of it. As I left that afternoon to drive along the muddy road to see the Chief I was in an absolute flurry of apprehension.

Despite my fears, I had to admit on arrival that Chief arap Sang, with his quietly spoken manner and compassionate eyes *did* appear to be a very nice man. He did not seem angry with me. In fact his greeting could not have been more courteous. By the time we reached his private office I really did not know what to think.

'You are happy in our country?' he inquired, indicating that I should take a seat.

'Oh yes, very happy,' I assured him.

His gaze was penetrating. 'That is good. Now, as you see, we are completely private here. You can tell me the truth and you need not be afraid of me. I want you to say whose baby you have in the house.'

'Whose baby?' I echoed more bewildered than ever.

'Yes. You see I know that arap Rob's own baby could not live for it was cursed. And I know that you are looking after another baby for him which is very kind of you, but still, in case there are problems later, you had better just tell me the name of the real father.'

The penny dropped. 'No, no Chief,' I cried, 'the baby

in my house is truly arap Rob's own child and his name is Kipngeno.'

He looked at me sternly, shaking his head. 'Impossible! Arap Rob's baby was cursed.'

'That is correct,' I told him. 'Arap Rob's baby *was* cursed. He became very sick and almost died. But, you know there is a power greater than the power of the witch-doctors. The Lord Jesus healed that baby and he is now well and strong and growing bigger every day.'

If it had simply been my word against the weight of Chief arap Sang's experience I wouldn't have had a hope in the world of convincing him, but providentially he decided to come and see the child for himself. One look at Kipngeno was enough to convince him. 'Well right enough, this is the very child,' he gasped. The resemblance was undeniable. From the depth of his forehead to the set of his chin, Kipngeno was the spitting image of his father.

We sat in my living-room for quite some time after that, discussing how this miracle of survival had taken place. Chief arap Sang was very impressed by the fact that Christians believed in a God strong enough to counteract the evil effects of a curse. He listened thoughtfully to everything the Dispensary Evangelist had to say; and I like to think that the whole incident played a significant part in his spiritual development. Throughout my time in Kipsigis he was a true and faithful friend to the children and me, and some years later, to my great delight, he came to know the Lord for himself.

At the time, however, I could only marvel at the wonderful way in which yet again God was using the children to reveal something of Himself. It seemed a further confirmation of the pattern of outreach that had been laid upon my heart. Already the children were opening doors for the gospel. How could I ever have doubted that God's anointing was upon the work!

Some months passed and the time came for me to return to Scotland for my first furlough. The five children, by this stage, were all well and strong enough to leave my home, which was a good thing, for there was no one to care for them in my absence. It was satisfying to give Chepkirui, Kipkoech and Kipkirui back to their parents and to know that I had fulfilled my role as far as they were concerned. But I felt as if I was abandoning Kipngeno and Chebet. Kipngeno's father did not seem able to meet the emotional needs of his small son and I sensed a similar disability in Chebet's stepmother - which made parting from these two little ones exceptionally painful.

Had my children's work in Litein come to an end? In one sense it seemed to have served its purpose. A seed had been planted in people's minds which was already beginning to bear fruit. The need for a work among children was being recognized in the wider community, and just before I left, I heard some very good news: I had applied for permission to live on an empty Mission Station in Ogada, a village near Kisumu, but the Church Leaders decided instead to open an orphanage there under African management, which was a much better idea.

On my return to Litein Dispensary, I was assigned to visit the Ogada Home regularly to check on the health of the children. To my great joy I was also given official permission to look after needy children myself.

My official 'side-line' took off like a bush-fire. Almost before I knew it, I had fourteen children in the house. Kipngeno and Chebet were amongst them. Just as I had feared, they had been badly neglected whilst I was away. Chebet had become so malnourished, she could no longer walk, while Kipngeno's whole personality had altered. In place of the happy out-going little fellow I had left, I found a scrawny withdrawn two-year-old, obviously suffering from the lack of a mother figure. His father was keen that I should take him back. The other children came for similar reasons - many through the intervention of Chief arap Sang, who was now lending his whole-hearted support to the children's work in his district. Those such as Cheruiyot and Chepkoech, whose mothers had died, were to stay with me long-term, whereas little ones like Kibet and Kipkirui, who had been born prematurely, would go home once they had gained enough weight to survive. Naturally I was delighted at the way the work had developed, but the tension between my responsibilities at the Dispensary and caring for the children became greater than ever.

'Please pray that God will send a person of His choice to take charge of the Dispensary because I'm not doing it too well, 'I wrote to Jean in June 1975, 'I feel *very* old and very tired and just can't rustle up the energy to do as much work as I want to any more.'

By the time the orphanage in Ogada was officially opened by the leader of the Africa Inland Church, twenty-four children had passed through my house. God *had* sent me help in the Dispensary in the form of two volunteers from the Campus Crusade Agape programme. Still I was concerned about the future of the work. It was great having Sylvia and Betty, but they were in Litein on a temporary basis, and almost every week I was hearing of another child in need of special care. My house was not big enough - my allowance did not go far enough - my body could not do enough. What would happen when I next went home on furlough?

'There was an old woman who lived in a shoe,' I found myself humming wryly one evening as I prepared to give Kibet his ten o'clock feed, 'who had so many children she didn't know what to do...'

There was a knock on the door. 'Come in!' I called. I already knew who it was. Since my return to Litein a new Evangelist had come to the Dispensary - a dedicated young Pastor called Matthew Korir. Matthew totally shared my vision for children's work and supported me, not just on a spiritual level, but on a practical level as well. He was even prepared to wipe noses and change nappies, and often, after his duties in the Dispensary were finished, would come round to help me with the ten o'clock feeds. Normally we spent the time chatting over the days events, but tonight, as we sat in the living-room with a baby apiece on our laps, he seemed unusually thoughtful.

'Is there anything the matter, Matthew?' I asked.

He reached out for a feeding bottle and inserted it into Kipkirui's mouth. 'It is strange,' he said,' but this morning when I was praying, I felt that the Lord was calling me to help you full-time with this work.'

My heart leapt. I knew that Matthew would not make that sort of statement lightly. 'Matthew, you know as well as I do that what this home needs is an African manager and I would like nothing better than for you to take on the job,' I said eagerly, 'but an appointment like that would be in the hands of the Regional Church Council. It's certainly not the sort of thing we could organize ourselves. All we can do is pray that God will bring it to pass.'

'You are right,' he nodded, a slight shadow crossing his face. 'And please, when you are praying, pray for Priscilla also.'

Priscilla was Matthew's girlfriend, a beautiful young Christian woman, with a quiet gentle nature. I knew that Matthew loved her and longed to marry her. Before he could do so, though, he had to raise some money. Priscilla was an educated girl, a Bible school graduate, and her father would expect a dowry. For months Matthew had been saving as much as he could from his salary.

'I would like Priscilla to share my call,' he said quietly.

I felt for him. Everyone who would be a true disciple of Christ is bound to come up against such difficulties between the Father's will and the natural desire of his/her own heart and they can be agonising.

A few days later Priscilla herself came to visit me. I knew as soon as she walked through the door that she too had something on her mind, but typically it was some time before she took me into her confidence. At last she found the words. As she had been praying and reading her Bible over the past few weeks, she told me, she had begun to wonder whether the Lord was calling her to work with children. She could not help feeling it might be His will for her to help me full-time. There was just one problem - Matthew. What would he think of her giving up her work in the Dispensary in order to work with the children?

God seemed to be stage-managing affairs so beautifully that I could scarcely contain my excitement. Yet at the same time something told me that His plan was still in its earliest most vulnerable stages and that to speak out of turn could do irreparable damage. With the utmost difficulty, I held myself in check. 'Let's just keep praying that the Lord will make his will for the future of the Children's Home abundantly clear,' I said.

Despite my past experiences of God's goodness and of the perfection of his timing, the next development all but took my breath away. Unknown to me, Chuck Kinzer, an A.I.M. missionary who had been very involved in the opening of the Children's Home in Ogada, had approached the Bishop of the Africa Inland Church on my behalf suggesting that he should write to *Stichting Redt een Kind*, a Dutch organization*, and ask them to consider financing another Children's Centre in Litein. At the time the letter had seemed a very long shot. Up to this point the foundation had been mainly involved in sponsoring orphans and older children, hence their contribution to Ogada. It seemed very unlikely that the Dutch board would agree to put my fourteen babies on to their books. But to everyone's amazement the general secretary, Mrs. Rookmaaker, responded very positively to the Bishop's request. The Lord had given her a burden for the needs of small babies as well as children, she explained, and only a few days prior to the arrival of his letter she had been wishing that more could be done for them!

'She's going to discuss funding at the next Board Meeting on the 10th March,' Chuck told me.

The final result was far beyond anything I could ever

---

*The English translation of the name is *Save a Child Foundation*. In order to avoid confusion with *Save the Children*, an entirely different organisation, the Dutch version has been used.

have hoped for. Not only was *Stichting Redt een Kind* willing to send me 200 Kenyan shillings a month per baby but they were also willing to contribute 650 shillings each month towards the salary of an African Manager - with one proviso. He had to be a married man.

The Regional Church Council held a lengthy committee meeting to determine who should be given the post. The discussion lasted for hours. In the end the chairman came to me, an expression of satisfaction, tinged with uncertainty on his face.

'Katie,' he asked, 'did you have anyone in particular in mind for this job?'

'Well, yes,' I admitted, 'I did. But I didn't want to say anything about it. It seemed better simply to trust God that the committee would appoint the man of His choosing, so, tell me, what is your decision?'

'Write down the name of the person you had in mind, and then I will tell you,' the Pastor said.

I scribbled it quickly on the corner of a notebook.

'The person we felt to be the man of God's choice was Matthew Korir.'

'And that is the very name I have written here.'

'So you have confirmed our decision!' He rubbed his hands together in delight, but almost immediately uncertainty gained the upper hand: 'But how can it be right? Our friends in Holland have agreed to pay the salary of a married man and as for Matthew Korir, he is still single.'

'Sit down,' I said, as soothingly as an all but overwhelming sense of elation would allow. 'I have a little piece of information for you about Matthew.'

'Matthew Korir is about to be married!'

The news took everyone by storm - including Matthew. *About* to be married? How could he hope to raise the money for his dowry so quickly?

But God had everything under control. A gift arrived from Scotland with instructions that it should go towards Matthew's marriage settlement. Another gift followed. Putting these together with an advance in salary Matthew was able to pay off his dowry in a matter of weeks and on 20th April, the long-awaited wedding took place. Radiant with happiness, the young couple posed for photographs on the lawn outside my house, surrounded by the babies for whom God had called them to care.

Needless to say their joy in discovering that they had individually been led in the same direction had known no bounds. The sense of a joint calling had given their marriage and their ministry the firmest possible foundation.

In the months which followed that foundation was put to the test. A large six-bedroom house on the Mission Station became available. Matthew and Priscilla moved in and before long each of those bedrooms was occupied by needy children. It was not the sort of responsibility many young couples would care to shoulder right at the start of their married life, but God gave them the grace to adjust and do the job superbly well:

'We do thank God very many times for this young couple who truly love the Lord Jesus,' I wrote in a prayer letter, 'and because of His love within them they also love the children. Matthew is now the Manager of the Children's Centre and the father of the children. Priscilla runs the house and is their warm-hearted mother. I'm the nurse. I take care of any babies who are sick in my home and also teach basic child-care to the African girls who help Priscilla.'

In July Mrs. Rookmaaker, accompanied by her husband and children, came to visit the Children's Centre. A crowd of bright-eyed children with fabulous smiles and outstretched hands came rushing out to greet her. Later, over a celebratory meal, Matthew explained that they fell into several categories: there were those who were truly orphans with neither father nor mother living who would remain in the home until they were eighteen; there were semi-orphans, such as Kipngeno who would stay until the one parent living could see fit to take them back; there were premature babies who would be returned to their mothers once they weighed ten pounds; and there were children, such as Chebet, with severe malnutrition who would stay as long as necessary for them to regain their health.

The visit was a great success. Socially, as far as the children and staff were concerned, it was the highlight of the year. And, in terms of the development of the home, it was a watershed. Mrs. Rookmaaker pronounced herself satisfied with what was being done and gave the Children's Centre official recognition.

God had fulfilled a vision. Just as He had promised in those early days when I had been caring for Kipngeno and Co. out of my missionary allowance, the work had expanded, developing in a manner I could never have foreseen. Money, buildings, and (most important of all!) personnel - all had been supplied. Even the Dispensary had been taken care of. Betty and Sylvia had left but Faith and Diana, two further volunteers from the Agape programme, had come to take their place.

In the after-glow of Mrs. Rookmaaker's visit, I sat with Matthew and Priscilla in my living-room and the wonder of God's planning struck us afresh. He was the everlasting Father, the one who knew the end from the beginning. What security! And at the back of my mind a little voice amended the second line of a familiar nursery rhyme:

There was an old woman who lived in a shoe
She'd a great many children...
but God knew what to do!

CHAPTER TEN

PARTNERS TOGETHER

Over the next nine months sixty-four children were sheltered for varying lengths of time beneath the roof of the Children's Centre. Fourteen premature babies thrived and went home to their families, while twenty-two children recovered from the effects of severe malnutrition. For many of them the medical outlook had been very poor. Severe kwashiorkor causes skin loss, and where a child has lost skin from over twenty-five percent of its body, there is, according to the medical text-books, little hope of survival. Whilst having the greatest respect for medical opinion, Matthew, Priscilla and I firmly believed prayer could alter the natural course of events. We never considered the death of a child to be inevitable, but instead met together every evening to commend any sick children individually to the care of a loving heavenly Father, trusting Him for healing.

One day three English doctors from the Government Ministry of Health and an official from the British High Commissioner's Office paid the home an unexpected visit. Word had reached them that children with a very high degree of malnutrition were recovering in the Children's Centre. 'We would like details of your nutrition programme,' they told me as the children surrounded them, smiling angelically, their big black eyes shining like stars. It gave me the greatest satisfaction imaginable to be able to tell them that there was nothing at all remarkable about the diet in the Children's Centre, but that we *did* believe in referring each individual case to the Great Physician. *That*, as they could see for themselves, enabled us to defy the statistics.

By this stage Matthew, accompanied by James and Joshua, another young Pastor, had arrived and was able to enlighten our visitors further as to the spiritual principles upon which the Children's Centre operated. Realizing that it was well after one o'clock and that they would need something to eat before they left, I began to prepare a meal. I had just tossed a mixture of fish, cheese and milk into the pressure cooker and handed James the potato peeler, when two of the Church Leaders came through the door.

'Are all these people connected with the Children's Centre?' the government official inquired a little bemusedly.

'Well, it's like this,' I summed up. 'The two Pastors are here to divert you, while James helps me to throw a late lunch together for you, and the Church Leaders are here in case you take it into your heads to bully me.'

This remark was greeted with a roar of laughter.

'We must remember to get into a nasty bullying mood before we come again,' the official observed, winking at his companions.

They could hardly have forgotten their visit to Litein in a hurry. It was that sort of set-up! A home constantly in a state of organised chaos, with bright-eyed children peering round every corner and an entire village community on the door-step.

Because I was so very happy and had such a wonderful working relationship with Matthew and Priscilla (one of the most joyful occasions of my life was the day I delivered their first child - tiny Jean Chebet) the last thing I wanted to do was to face up to the fact that by the beginning of January 1977, I had a health problem. I felt constantly exhausted. When Matthew, with his usual sensitivity, noticed that I was not myself and asked if anything was wrong, I put him off with a half-truth which he seemed to accept. A couple of months later, however, he brought the subject up again, this time in Dr. Bill's hearing.

'There is something the matter with Katie. As for me, I think she needs a check-up,' he pronounced to my consternation.

Dr. Bill, being Dr. Bill, insisted on an immediate consultation.

'Any symptoms? Pain? Nausea?'

There was no getting out of it; I had to tell him the truth.

'I'm afraid it is going to mean surgery,' he informed me gently, after a thorough examination.

I had the operation - a hysterectomy - a couple of days later. Dr. Bill was about to leave Kenya for the Comores, so things had to happen fast. How greatly I appreciated God's provision of so skilful and godly a surgeon as I lay there in theatre! The last thing I heard before I drifted into unconsciousness was his voice, praying that I would be fully restored to health and that God would continue to use me in His service. I woke up fully assured from the Lord that it was not yet time for me to depart this world for the next! Despite post-operative pain, my heart was full of joy. I knew that He was in charge and held my future in His hands.

My three-month long convalescence was a transition

period. The loving care which my Kipsigis friends show-
ered upon me seemed like the mellow golden rays of an
October sun. During the six weeks I spent in Kijabe a car-
load of them, including Matthew and Priscilla made the
long journey from Litein faithfully every Sunday to visit
me. When Dr. Bill finally gave me permission to return
home under strict instructions not to do any work whatsoever, they ensured that I followed those instructions to
the letter. It was so good to be back: to watch the children
playing on the lawn, to allow Priscilla to coax me into
eating, to bask in the warmth of so much loving concern.
But, there was no escaping it; the breath of change was in
the air. As soon as I was strong enough, I was due to return
to Scotland and I knew deep down that it was time to
move from Litein.

There was a huge lump in my throat at my farewell
party. I was presented with a mat made out of black and
white goatskins sewn closely together - a symbol of
motherhood, Matthew told me ... and of my oneness with
my Kipsigis brothers and sisters in the Lord!

Shivering, a couple of days later, I stepped out into the
less than tropical temperatures of Heathrow airport.

A bemused, yellow-faced figure wearing clothes fash-
ionable around the time that Santa Claus was in nappies
- that is the stereotyped image of a missionary on
furlough and, from the outset, it has been a stereotype
I've tried to avoid. As the child of a King, I do not think
for one minute that God intends me to go around looking
like everybody's poor relation. I constantly praise and
thank Him for the wonderful network of caring friends
and relatives which He has given me in Scotland and
further afield who have responded so sensitively and
lovingly to my needs. I have never had any problems with

my wardrobe, despite the fact that changes of climate combined with changes in my own shape and size have sometimes necessitated building it up again from scratch.

Obviously readjusting to Western culture is far more than a question of clothes and appearance. Again I have been singularly blessed in having a friend such as Jean, who, as soon as she hears I am coming home, makes a point of gathering together a selection of Christian books and news items, to help me get abreast of the things that have been going on in my absence. Still, it would be wrong for me to suggest that I am able to swing from one culture to another with the ease of a trapeze artist.

The main problem centres round the fact that I usually come home at a low ebb physically, which means that, for the first few months at least, the most ordinary everyday things seem to require a huge effort and it is all too easy to lose a sense of proportion. Magazines and news items only prepare me for major developments; they do not prepare me for the fact that potatoes aren't being sold loose any more, or that the bus that I am supposed to catch has changed colour, or that J. R. Ewing is a character in a soap opera and not a member of parliament. I have returned from a supermarket empty-handed, missed my connection and made an utter fool of myself, as a result of trivialities such as these. The yellow face, frumpish clothes and battered suitcase can all be circumvented - but it would seem that for every returning missionary there is bound to be a degree of disorientation.

There is also bound to be deputation. Deputation is what missionaries do on furlough (apart from spending time with their families and having a rest). It means travelling around speaking to various Christian groups. The object is to keep prayer-partners up to date with what has been going on, and to encourage people to support the work of the Mission.

The first time I came home on furlough, the very word 'deputation' was enough to make me wish I was back in Kenya. I was totally unused to speaking in public, a fact that must have been painfully obvious to all those who had the misfortune to listen to me. At my first meeting, I stammered my way through my report, so overcome by nerves that I forgot to read the Scriptures and at meeting number two, I forgot to pray. Meeting number three was an eight minute slot at the Faith Mission conference. By this stage I was so unglued about the whole business that I decided to fast and pray all day in preparation.

The discipline probably did me good spiritually, but the effect on my subsequent performance was negligible. For the longest thirty seconds of my life-time, I stood before a sea of expectant faces, struggling to gather my thoughts, before finally being sucked under by a current of hopelessness and retiring from the platform in tears.

Fortunately I had not come to the meeting alone. Jan Walkinshaw, the Scottish secretary of A.I.M. (and the person who had first planted the idea of missionary work in my mind) was with me. I cannot quite remember what she said, as she chauffeured me home, but it was soothing and sensible and removed something of the immediate sting from the occasion.

I was staying with George and Jean at the time. One look at my face as I slumped in through the door was enough to put them in the picture.

'Look Katie, if you can't do the thing, don't do it!' George said.

'But I *have* to,' I wailed.

'No you don't,' he insisted. '*You* don't have to do

anything. Remember how you stopped smoking!'

And once again I discovered that the answer lay in a simple 'do it for me' prayer, uttered from the depths of my own weakness. George prayed with me, asking God to take over my mouth. And He did. From that time on I was free from the fear of public-speaking. I spoke about my work at a prayer gathering in Sandyford Church the following Saturday night and actually enjoyed it.

Basically, I have been enjoying deputation ever since. At times it can be draining: like the proverbial troubles, meetings never seem to come singly. 'I don't know how you keep going!', Maureen, a friend I stayed with on deputation in Ireland used to say, as she plied me with mugs of tea while I lay soaking in the bath. The answer was simple. The kind of practical concern which would manifest itself in something as apparently insignificant as a cup of tea in the bath, was constantly recharging my batteries.

Yes, travelling from place to place night after night did sometimes drain me. More often than not, though, the warm response of the particular group of people to whom I was speaking spurred me on, making me appreciate afresh the great joy of sharing with my partners in mission - for partners they are, those groups of people meeting week by week or month by month to pray for the work. Without them, it simply would not be possible.

During my furlough of 1977, deputation took me all over Scotland, and further afield - to the islands, the Highlands, the Lowlands and even the Netherlands! I brought a set of slides with me and everywhere I went I was touched by the degree of interest expressed in the children. Of course some might say that the general warmth of sympathy and good-will towards my work was rooted in sentimentality; (who, after all could resist a picture of Kibet and Kipkirui on opposite sides of a pair of weighing scales? Or of Chebet, rubbing her legs in a sunbeam?) but although babies do directly appeal to the emotions, I could never dismiss the level of interest which I encountered as mere sentimentality. In my view, it most frequently bore the hallmark of a genuine spiritual stirring - a response to the realization that these children were precious to God.

I make this claim on the basis of the quality of that response. It seemed that so many who heard the story of the Children's Centre wanted to support the work; not just with a once-off monetary gift - a token, salving the conscience - but thoughtfully and prayerfully and often at great personal cost. The giving of small fellowships never ceases to amaze me. It is not possible, of course, even to begin to list the names of the groups and individuals who helped in this way. Still, in the knowledge that God has Himself a complete record of every loving sacrificial action carried out in His name, I give a few examples.

I spoke at a meeting in Greenock. It was not a wealthy area, but before the final hymn a large collection was taken up for my work. The final hymn was sung, the minister pronounced the benediction - and nobody moved. I did not know what to think. And then from the back of the hall came a voice: 'Do you mind if we pass the plate again?'

On another occasion I spoke to a group of school-children in Lochgilphead. They clearly identified with the slides and wanted to do something to help equip the children's home. 'It has to be your own effort,' the headmaster told them - so they decided to have a sale of their own toys. Normally such sales realized about six or seven pounds but this sale was different: the children did not just give toys they had out-grown, but toys they were still playing with. One little fellow, himself from a very deprived background, insisted on placing his sole possession, a large rather moth-eaten teddy-bear, on the stall. I wept when I heard. In his letter, the headmaster enclosed a cheque for £120.

One final story: Mrs. MacKinnon was an elderly lady who regularly received my prayer letter. She had written to me, when I was in Kenya, asking for the names of any new children coming into the home. On returning to Scotland, I decided to pay her a visit. She was, I discovered, very seriously ill. 'But she will be absolutely delighted to see you,' her daughter assured me as she led the way to the bedroom.

Her mother was sitting up in bed, a frail figure, dozing against a mountain of pillows. Will she even recognize me, I wondered? I was in for a shock. Not only did Mrs. MacKinnon recognize me, she also recognized the pictures in my photograph album.

'Ah, there's Chepkemoi and there's Kendu. And there's dear little Kiprotich,' she murmured happily, pointing out each individual face with her wasted forefinger.

'But how can you tell?' I marvelled. It was the first time I had brought this particular set of prints to Scotland and there were no names in the album.

She looked at me with the matter-of-fact simplicity of those who, in the tradition of Brother Lawrence, continually practise the presence of God: 'He showed me their faces, as I prayed,' she said.

It was an inspiring example of prayer-partnership at

its most meaningful, and more than that, it seemed somehow to encapsulate the ideal of the Children's Centre. Governments, hospitals and official bodies of all kinds tend to deal in statistics and faceless generalisations. God deals with individuals and their specific needs. That is why it was so important to have people with a vision of His love relating on a daily basis to the children. And that is why Mrs. MacKinnon's prayer journey took her beyond the place of generalisations. She did not just pray that God would save and bless malnourished children; she prayed specifically - beautifully illustrating how the unique characteristics of each individual child are known to Him.

In the midst of all the comings and goings of my deputation programme, I did not have a great deal of time to reflect. Yet I knew it was important to do so; it is all too easy for those who serve the Lord 'officially' in a full-time capacity to become dry spiritually; to give their all in their sphere of service, and yet experience a sense of barrenness and confusion in their on-going relationship with Him. Books have been written about the subject - and in the small hours of the morning, as I tried to put my own spiritual house in order, it was through a book that God spoke to me, putting His finger fairly and squarely on a problem-area in my spiritual life, which until then I had been trying to ignore.

The book was a well-known Christian classic - *Something More* by Catherine Marshall. Catherine Marshall is probably my favourite Christian writer, and in the past her books had never failed to inspire me. So it was with the first two chapters of this one, as she shared insights on the nature of praise and the importance of recognizing God at the centre of everything; I found myself joyfully assenting to every word. But as I embarked upon chapter three, entitled 'Forgiveness: The Aughts and the Anys', I ceased to be comfortably inspired and became uncomfortably convicted.

'For years,' Catherine Marshall wrote, 'I attached a condition to my forgiveness: if the other person saw the error of his ways, was properly sorry, and admitted his guilt, then - yes, as a Christian, I was obligated to forgive him. Finally I had to face the fact that this was my fixed set of conditions, not Christ's. For He said, "Forgive if ye have aught against any..." '*

Over the years, I realized, I too had stored up a great many aughts against anys! There had been a broken relationship in Bible College days, the fracas with the hospital authorities over the abortion issue and more recently a series of personality clashes, some major, some minor, which had seemed to be part and parcel of my getting the children's work off the ground. I still had a fiery temper, acting and speaking on impulse. Yet now I saw that regardless of the rights and wrongs of all these situations, I had to forgive, actively releasing all those who had crossed me from my judgement.

To a certain extent I side-stepped the issue. My daily round of activities mitigated against an in-depth spiritual spring-cleaning operation such as was suggested in the book. Therefore I did not reap the full spiritual benefits. I fully assented to the principle, though, and made some progress in releasing people from my harsh judgements of the past. I also grew in self-awareness, discovering that for me judging others was a defence mechanism which helped me to feel less inferior myself. Stripped of the

*Catherine Marshall, *Something More*, Hodder and Stoughton Ltd, London, 1974, pp 48-49.

right to put other people in the wrong, I would come face to face with my own imperfections. I must try to remember that when I get back to Kenya, I resolved.

It was June 1978. I had fulfilled my last speaking engagement, had spent a last couple of weeks quietly at home with Mum and Dad, had packed the last pair of plastic pants into a corner of my luggage and was ready for off. After a full year in Scotland, I was itching to get back to work. There had been such encouraging developments in my absence. Under the sponsorship of the *Stichting Redt een Kind* foundation more and more children's homes were opening up. It was at once satisfying and humbling to realize that despite my mistakes, the Lord had used the work in Litein to make the Church more aware of the plight of orphaned children. There had even been an article about the development of the work in the October/November edition of the Mission magazine.

Katie is at present on leave and when she returns she expects to be assigned as nurse 'at large' to the Children's Centres. This will broaden the scope of her ministry ... In years gone by eight out of ten babies died. Now it's the other way round...

I had read the words with a thrill of anticipation. Now, as I sat in Heathrow airport, I realized that despite the pain of those goodbyes, which certainly did not get any easier with the passing of time, I was looking forward to my new assignment; I wanted to serve God, working with children, more than anything else in the world...

CHAPTER ELEVEN

A BATTLE OF WILLS

'We have decided to give you a second chance.' The statement, made in a dry matter-of-fact tone, hit me like a physical blow. I had come to the Church Office to discuss my new assignment. Right from the beginning of the interview, I had sensed a touch of frost in the air, but this was the very last thing I had expected.

'What do you mean - a second chance?'

'Well according to our information,' the personnel official elaborated briefly, 'you have spent the last four years fighting with Church Leaders.'

'But that is simply not true! I had a very good relationship with the Church Leaders in Litein. They were in and out of my home all the time. A group of them even came to the airport yesterday to meet me!'

I might as well have saved my breath. The decision had already been taken.

'You are being assigned to Mulango Dispensary,' my superior explained. 'It's been shut for two years and the Church Leaders there want it reopened.'

My heart sank into my ankles. If the Church Office had got together with the *Wazee* (or Church Leaders) and tried to dream up the assignment least likely to appeal to me humanly-speaking, they couldn't have done a better job. They had assigned me to an out-patient Dispensary and in terms of job-fulfilment, out-patient Dispensaries came bottom of my list! Yet what could I say? If, as it seemed, the matter was closed, there was no point in further protest.

I left Nairobi in the unhappiest imaginable frame of mind, and the one hundred and fifty kilometre journey east into the Kitui region - a particularly arid and impoverished part of Kenya - did nothing to improve it. Eventually my driver, a charming girl, who kilometre after kilometre, had chatted cheerfully, deposited me at Mulango and drove off with a wave of her hand.

Morosely I looked around me. In spite of everything I had to admit that the place had character. It had been taken over from the Leipzig Lutheran Mission in 1915 and the missionary dwellings - four in all - were arranged around a patch of grass against a brilliant background of pink and purple bougainvillea. One was very old, dating right back to its German origin in 1895.

Nor was there any denying the warmth and the sincerity with which I was welcomed. Geneva, one of the longest-serving missionaries on the field, promptly and enthusiastically took me under her wing.

'We are absolutely delighted to have you here,' she said, slipping her arm about my waist and leading me over to her spotlessly neat home. 'The Akamba people have been waiting so long for this Dispensary!'

I stiffened, too hurt and mixed-up to make any pretence of responding graciously. I had nursed my anger all the way to Mulango; together with a sense of shame at my inability to rise above it, Catherine Marshall-style, and demonstrate a spirit of forgiveness. I did not want to open a Dispensary. I had been called by God to work with children. The Authorities had seemed at one time to have recognized that. Yet now I felt labelled a failure. How dare they! I was angry, but I was also very confused. Why had this happened? Could I have mistaken God's leading? It was all so unfair ... so terribly unfair ...

I felt more depressed than ever when I saw the Dispensary. The mud-brick building with its corrugated iron roof had been taken over by wild-life. Bats - thousands of them - had made their home in the rafters, saturating the ceiling with urine, while down below the medical records had been half-eaten by termites. The smell was indescribable. 'If the people are as keen to get the Dispensary reopened as you say they are, why has this building not been cleaned out?'

I demanded. Geneva did her best to calm me down. Of course nobody was expecting the Dispensary to reopen immediately, she reasoned. There would have to be a meeting with the *Wazee* to decide the best way to go about it.

For the next few weeks I hung around waiting for something to happen. I wrote letters and got to know the other Mulango missionaries - Bertha, Nancy, the Bainbridges. Like Geneva, they all had a job. I was the only one with nothing to do.

Finally the summons came; I was to attend a committee meeting the following day. Since I was back to square one as far as my language study was concerned, not knowing a word of Kikamba beyond the elementary greetings, Clarence Bainbridge came with me to translate.

What a difference between the *Wazee* here and the ones in Kipsigis, I thought with a wave of nostalgia! The Kipsigis pastors had always made every effort to communicate with me directly whether I liked what they had to say or not; but everything these Akamba leaders said was directed towards Clarence. I was dispatched to make tea while they discussed my fate.

I suppose that is all they think I'm good for, I thought darkly as I trotted off, returning some twenty minutes later to dispense the steaming brew.

Clarence cleared his throat. 'The Church Leaders have decided that you are to open the Dispensary. It should be cleaned and painted and medicine should be bought as quickly as possible.'

'Tell them,' I said, 'that there is precisely £22 in the Dispensary account, which means that by the time I've bought the paint, there won't be enough left over to buy an aspirin! Tell them that it is *their* Dispensary so they have got to share the responsibility of getting it open.'

There was a brief interchange during which the men raised their cups to their lips and looked anything but happy.

'So what do they say?' I asked.

'Yes, well, they want me to tell you that you didn't put enough sugar in the tea ...'

I left the meeting, my self-confidence as low as it had been in a long time. Could it be that the unfavourable report about me had been accurate after all, I wondered? Had I been deluding myself in Litein? Imagining that I was getting on well with the national leaders, when all the time they were placing a very different interpretation on my behaviour? After all confrontation was not the African way, and at times I *had* undoubtedly confronted people. Outspoken as I was, would I be able to control my tongue any better in this new assignment? Did I even want to? The thought of single-handedly opening that indescribably filthy Dispensary and scrounging around for medicines filled me with bleak dismay.

On July 21st, Mrs. Rookmaaker arrived in Kenya. She had come to visit the six Children's Centres which were receiving financial support from Holland. Originally there had been talk of my driving her around, but I had heard nothing further about that, and was actually due to attend an executive medical committee meeting in Nairobi. Mrs. Rookmaaker, however, had other ideas. She made it quite clear to all concerned that she had come with the understanding that I would be accompanying her on her travels. So where was I?

The Church Office hastily instructed me to skip the medical committee meeting and join her on safari.

That trip was such an encouragement to me! From start to finish God used it to lift my spirits. First there was the wonderful joy of being with Matthew, Priscilla and the children (forty-four in all) again; of seeing little Jean Chebet and George Kiplangat, their three month old son; of meeting with the Church Leaders. They came, en masse, to greet us. Each one made a speech welcoming Mrs. Rookmaaker, and each one went on to say at length how much they wished I could have stayed at Litein.

From Litein we made our way to the five other homes. To my amazement the African Managers, North, South, East and West, welcomed me with open arms. Everywhere we went I was invited to come and work as much as possible with the children.

Our final port of call was the Bishop's residence in Kangundo. Drawing to a halt outside his impressive front door, I felt extremely apprehensive. It was the Bishop who, ultimately, was responsible for all missionary assignments. He would know the reason I had been taken

out of children's work and sent to Mulango and now I
half-expected him to chew me up and fill the holes in his
teeth with me for daring to accompany Mrs. Rookmaaker
under the Children's Centre umbrella.

Again, I was in for a pleasant surprise. The Bishop
could not have been kinder or more reassuring. He had
wanted the Dispensary opened in Mulango because the
Wazee had been requesting it for so long, he explained.
But there was no question of his putting me out of
children's work.

'I have been out of the country for three and a half
months and there has been some misunderstanding at the
Church Office,' he said. 'I know that you work well with
the *Wazee*. I also know that you always work with
children so that is exactly what I want you to do.'

One of the first things I did when I got back to
Mulango was to write a long exuberant letter to Jean:

'Can you imagine the loving kindness of the Lord?' I
marvelled. 'Until the trip I was in such a dither wondering
whether to resign or not, because it seemed to me from
what I'd been told on my arrival that I was a complete
misfit. God used the African people - each one of them -
to show that all the while their eyes had *not* been on me,
but on God who could work *even* through me. This
wonderful truth has shaken a lot of things into focus, I can
tell you.'

My new assignment seemed to be coming together at
last. Shortly after my interview with the Bishop, Dr. Bill
and Frank Frew, the Mission representative for the area,
came to Mulango to talk with the *Wazee*. As a result of
that meeting it was generally understood that, if the need
arose, I had permission to care for children in my own
home.

After that, however, I was back in the doldrums. August went by and September, with few positive developments. At one point frustration nearly got the better of me. It seemed so feeble to be sitting around waiting for something to happen. I felt I had had as much as I could take and decided to leave Mulango. Providentially, as I was lugging my suitcase over to my car, the Principal of the Bible College spotted me and persuaded me to think again.

'You'll see, something will be worked out very soon,' he assured me.

So I stayed. It was not willing obedience, still less was it joyful obedience. It was a grumbling, self-pitying sort of obedience, but deep down I still believed that God had called me to serve with the Africa Inland Mission and that until He showed me otherwise, any move on my part would be a move outside His will.

Eventually as September dragged to a close, I came to grips with the practicalities of reopening the Dispensary. Medicines were borrowed from Kijabe, volunteers helped me remove tin upon tin of bat's dung from the ceiling, and an opening date was fixed for 22nd October.

On the 18th October, a Bible College student came to my house. A woman in his village had recently died in childbirth, he told me. He was wondering who would take care of the children. The father was blind and the mother-in-law sick.

'It *does* sound like a very needy situation,' I agreed, and promised to investigate.

The man came from the Northern part of the Kitui region, from a tiny village called Tseikuru. It was too late to travel that day, but the following morning I picked up Gilbert Malusi, the manager of one of the Children's

Centres and we set off, bumping kilometre after kilometre along a narrow dusty bush road which threatened, in places, to disappear altogether.

Five long hours later we reached a dry river bed. On the other side we spotted a cluster of houses. Not a moment too soon! The village was so remote, I had the impression that one kilometre beyond it, we might fall off the edge of the world. It was a poor area - obviously. Roofs and walls were all in bad repair and there were few cattle to be seen.

We did not take long to locate the family. Outside the poorest, most dilapidated house of all, we found a blind man, an elderly woman and a lethargic group of malnourished children. As Malusi explained who we were and why we had come, the expression of despair lifted from the old woman's face and she jabbered away to him in Kikamba.

'She is too old and sick to look after these children,' Malusi told me. 'She wants us to take them.'

I looked at the children and nodded. There were five of them, ranging upwards in height like steps of stairs. The youngest seemed to be around two years old. But their mother had died in childbirth, I recalled. So what had happened to the baby? Glancing into the hut, I could see no sign of a sixth child. It must have died with her, I concluded. And then I heard a faint squeak from under a pile of rags by the door. I lifted them and gasped, for there, underneath was a tiny baby.

The wee soul was stiff with cold. Desperately I tried to massage some heat into the rigid arc of his body.

'There's no need to bother about him,' the grandmother informed me via Malusi. 'He's practically dead already.'

I could see for myself that there was very little hope. 'Tell her, we shall take him with us.'

The elderly woman shrugged.

'Just bury him at the side of the road when he dies,' was her response.

Against all the odds Philip did not die. Instead he became the first occupant of my new nursery. And a mere twenty-four hours later, on October 20th, another baby came to join him. Like Philip, John's mother had died in child-birth. John was followed by Mutui on October 21st and by Musembi on October 22nd, both suffering from very bad kwashiorkor. The influx of babies was totally un-planned and unexpected. On October 22nd, after three months of frustration, I found myself opening a Baby Home and a Dispensary almost simultaneously...

From the organisational point of view things devel-oped quite nicely from then on. Two very capable Akamba women came to work in the Dispensary and actually took over the day to day running of it, while in my home four Akamba girls helped me care for an ever increasing family of babies. When the time came to write my December prayer letter we had eleven little ones in the nursery:

'The children are, as usual, a very great joy and we have watched God at work healing wee sick bodies, providing for them, and a faint interest stirring up in the community because of them,' I wrote.

I only wished I could have been more positive about attitudes in the community. But sadly even my talk of a *faint interest* had a hollow ring. The truth of the matter was that as far as I could discern, the attitude of the *Wazee* towards the children was one of total apathy. In Litein I had always felt that the Church viewed the Children's Centre as part of their Christian witness in that area; the Leaders visited often, helping me in disciplinary matters and constantly supporting me with their prayers. In Mulango, however, I was lucky to see any member of the local Church community from one month to the next.

Perhaps this would not have galled me so much if everything had been running smoothly; but it wasn't. We had continual problems with water - leading to frequent bouts of diarrhoea and vomiting. And the New Year brought even greater trials:

'The "everyday" has become unbelievable,' I wrote to Jean in January. 'The children have passed from one illness to another - despite my every effort to keep them healthy. About two weeks ago they became extremely ill with very high fevers (one reached 105°F), coughs, chest problems, measles and chickenpox combined. You wouldn't believe how sick they are ...'

Four of them died. Even then, the *Wazee* did not come to pray with me. I was so upset about the whole business that I would quite happily have packed up my things and taken the children elsewhere. Surely God would not wish me to remain in Mulango under such uncaring leadership, I reasoned.

At the same time I was haunted by the story of Abraham and Isaac. All the trauma and heartache of the previous month had shown me more clearly than ever how very precious the children were to me. Did I set too much store by them, I wondered? How would I react if, like Abraham, I was required to sacrifice my Isaac? Would I be willing to leave children's work altogether and return to Scotland?

Since the beginning of the year I had been intending to get away for a week. I had booked myself into a very quiet Christian Guest House, and now with the remaining children well on the road to recovery, I realized how badly I needed that break - not just for physical but for spiritual reasons. I needed God to show me clearly what I was to do: whether, as I hoped, I was to leave Mulango with the children - or whether, as I dreaded, I was to leave Mulango without them?

That I should remain in Mulango was an option which I had preferred not to consider. So it came as a considerable blow to hear God say: 'Stay put!'

'But how can I stay there?' I argued. 'I just can't cope with the loneliness and the isolation any more.'

Again He spoke, gently rebuking my faithlessness, reaffirming my call. 'Take this child away and nurse it for me and *I* will give thee thy wages' (Exodus 2:9).

I returned to Mulango. The number of children in my home increased to fifteen and the practical everyday problems - shortage of water, gastric troubles, lack of space - persisted. The sense of isolation persisted too. Still, as far as I was concerned, I was staying - and, in time, I hoped, my relationship with the *Wazee* would improve.

The very last thing in this world I intended to do was to offend the Bishop. I had the greatest respect for the Bishop. He was a very gifted man, a fine administrator and in the past we'd always got on very well together. He had seemed genuinely to appreciate the need for children's work, and had given me every encouragement. But now a chance remark made by a third party created a false impression. It appeared that I was accusing him of dishonesty - something very serious to an African. His

attitude towards me changed. I could not understand it to
begin with, and by the time I learned the truth it was too
late for explanations; what ought to have been a small
matter, easily cleared up, had already mushroomed into
a major crisis. A letter had arrived ordering me to leave
Mulango by the end of November.

The reaction of the *Wazee* to that letter totally amazed
me. They threw up their hands in horror: 'But she cannot
be moved! She has started a valuable work with children!' Immediately they swung into action, calling an
emergency meeting of the Regional Church Council, as
a result of which a committee of men was appointed to
convey a letter of apology from me to the Bishop and to
intercede with him on my behalf.

They were brushed aside. It seemed that the Bishop
did not wish to discuss the matter. He had made up his
mind. I was leaving and there was nothing more to be said.

'But if she goes what will happen to the children?'
they asked.

'They will have to return to their villages,' he replied.
'Some may live. Some may die. It has always been like
that.'

I was deeply distressed when I heard about this. The
members of the delegation were most unhappy about it
also. 'As soon as he said those words, our hearts turned
to stone,' one of them told me afterwards. But it was not
just the Bishop's attitude towards the children which
upset them; they also resented the lack of consultation.
And the missionaries didn't like it either. Suddenly the
termination of my assignment became the battle-ground
on which wider issues of policy and Church politics were
being fought out. The Bishop had ordered me to move, but
the Church Leaders refused point blank to let me pack.

By the end of October I literally did not know if I was coming or going. '*No one* will agree that I should move ...' I wrote to Jean. 'And I must confess that I have not one microscopic wish to do so myself. I have put one enormous effort into obeying authority and will do so if I have to. You cannot imagine the reaction all this racket has produced - it is horrible.'

Horrible it was; and as in cases of such complexity, where many tensions and opposing interests are involved, it became increasingly difficult to sort out right from wrong, and even to find a guiding principle. My main concern was the children; the Church Office had written to Kijabe asking whether I could take my household there but the reply had been a regretful negative. There simply was not the accommodation.

One morning, when the affair was at its height and I was at my most wretched, Marjorie Bainbridge, my next-door neighbour, came into my living-room, her eyes alight with excitement: 'Katie,' she cried, 'I was praying for you this morning and the Lord has given me a message. You are to read Isaiah chapter fifty-four.'

I went into my bedroom, opened my Bible and it was as if Marjorie had delivered a letter hand-addressed to me by God:

Sing, O barren woman, thou that didst not bear; break forth into singing and cry aloud, thou that didst not travail with child: for more are the children of the desolate than the children of the married wife, saith the LORD.

Enlarge the place of thy tent, and let them stretch forth the curtains of thine habitations: spare not, lengthen thy cords, and strengthen thy stakes;

For thou shalt break forth on the right hand and on the left ...

I did not actually sing (my voice being of the corn-crake variety!) but I did cry tears of thankfulness. For I knew on reading it that God had not abandoned either me or the children, and that somehow there would be a way out of this tangled battle of wills. First and foremost I knew that I had to forget about Church politics and submit myself totally to God. Day after day I strove to hold on to that spirit of submission, while at the same time praying fervently with the other Mulango missionaries that the Bishop's attitude might be changed.

Sadly, I was soon to learn that the reconciliation between us would not take place this side of eternity. On a Sunday morning, shortly before the end of November, we received the stunning news that the Bishop had died.

The suddenness and the awesome finality of this happening shook the Church to the core, missionaries and Kenyans alike. Here was a solemn reminder that we have but a limited time on this earth to seek the glory of God; and that time spent in arguments and in-fighting is time wasted.

Soberly, some weeks later, the *Wazee* went to welcome the new Bishop.

To their inquiry about my position he answered as follows:

'Tell her to get on with the work which God has given her to do.'

CHAPTER TWELVE

ENCOUNTER WITH FAMINE

The story which I have just related was not an easy one to tell. In many ways I would have much preferred to skip over those first two years in Mulango with all their hurts and confusions. I have no wish to dwell upon them, still less to remember how far short I fell of my aspirations to forgive unconditionally and to handle difficulties in a Christ-like manner.

'Please pray that God will give me wisdom and also that I will stop talking about everything because it doesn't help,' I had written to Jean at the beginning when I was feeling so aggrieved at the way I had been treated; and later, when my sense of loneliness had reached a peak: 'Do I want to be like Jesus? Yes I do? Do I want to be forsaken by my friends and left on my very own with God? No I most certainly do not ...'

Times of trial and testing are times when very often our weary flesh and battered emotions cry out against the will of God, and certainly I did my fair share of that. It is partly for this reason that I have told the story of those early years in Mulango - as a record of the way God works *despite* our human shortcomings. But I have also told it as a reminder that, as Paul says in Ephesians 6:12:

> We wrestle not against flesh and blood, but against principalities, against powers ... against spiritual wickedness in high places.

For just as I am certain that it was indeed God's sovereign will for me to start a work amongst babies in Mulango, I am equally convinced that Satan did everything he could to prevent it. Looking back I shudder to think how close I came on several occasions to moving elsewhere. That I stayed put is no tribute to my personal faithfulness, but rather to the faithful prayers of my friends on my behalf and above all to the hand of a faithful God upon my life.

But why did God particularly want me in Mulango when I could have helped to care for children in half a dozen other places in Kenya? Of course I realize that it is never possible to fathom fully the depth and perfection of God's will, but one very basic answer to this question might be that God wished the Baby Home to be situated where the need was greatest.

Mulango is at the heart of the Kitui region, an area of 12,000 square miles of very poor land. Most of the half-a-million people who live off it are small farmers, growing maize, sorghum, cow peas and beans for home consumption. They depend on their crops for survival. When things are going well the rains come in December and in April, the crops grow and there is food in the pot. When the rains do not come, the crops fail, and there are food-shortages.

In 1980 I went home briefly to be with my family while Mum went into hospital for an operation on her hip. I returned to Mulango to find that the October rains had failed and that most of the basic food stuffs - flour, maize, rice, salt and sugar - were missing from the shops.

It was my first experience of famine.

On this occasion the food-shortages did not last more than six months; but that was quite long enough to show me how desperately vulnerable the people were. They had nothing to fall back on. With no maize in the fields and no money to buy any, they simply went hungry. Children with hair rusty red from protein deficiency or stomachs bloated by lack of food were a common sight.

I could only admit the very worst cases - little ones such as two-year-old Ngemba, who came into the Baby Home suffering from gross malnutrition. She weighed thirteen pounds, most of her skin was peeling off and she had TB.

The hard-pressed doctor from the Government Hospital was angry with me when he came to examine her.

'You must have some idea how busy I am at the hospital,' he snapped. 'Yet you have hauled me over here on a fool's errand. I can do nothing for the child. She is dying - anyone can see that.'

I dropped into the hospital to see him five months later and he was forced to change his tune. 'Do you know who that is?' I inquired, producing a picture of a little girl proudly modelling a string of coloured beads.

He shook his head. 'It's Ngemba. Remember - the child who wasn't supposed to live.'

'Well, I'll be blowed!' For a moment he studied the photograph, then pronounced with a sheepish grin: 'From now on I'll diagnose and you pray and we'll call it combination medicine.'

But for every story with a happy ending such as this, there were a multitude of tragedies. There is no happy ending to a famine situation - just a terrible sense of helplessness in the face of widespread human misery.

Why does it happen? Who is to blame? How may it be prevented? These are questions with political and economic implications beyond the scope of this book and I do not pretend to be able to tackle them. Personally, though, I find myself seeing the physical horror of famine as one symptom of that wider spiritual famine which drives men and women to place material gain and the wielding of worldly power at the top of their list of priorities. I read the Gospels and note how Jesus healed the sick and fed a hungry crowd, thus showing His concern for people's physical needs and His desire to meet them. But the things of the spirit were always His primary concern. He never led His disciples to believe that He had come to solve the problems of this world overnight; His was a heavenly Kingdom, based on a personal relationship with God. As then, so today He constantly challenges us to think in terms of relationships; our relationship with God and our relationship with other people.

And the Church has been given the task of revealing this Christ to the nations - a challenging, redeeming, compassionate, healing Saviour. Just as my doctor friend at the Government Hospital came to recognize the value of combining medicine with prayer, so we must recognize the need to combine prayer with action. As our Lord walked this earth He cared for people, body, mind and spirit. Today, as we walk the earth proclaiming His Name, I believe that He longs to channel His redemptive power through us into the situations of darkness and despair from which, perhaps in the awareness of our human inadequacy, we naturally tend to shy away.

During the famine in Kitui there were many unfed, and apparently uncared for bodies. I grieved for them. At the same time, if I had needed proof that it was right to be in Mulango I had it then. The Baby Home was able to provide shelter for children who would otherwise have died, and food for quite a number of impoverished families. This was made possible by the generosity of organisations, such as *Stichting Redt een Kind*, of Churches, of concerned community groups, and of many many individuals who gave until it hurt. It seemed to me then as if God had brought the Home into being as one expression of His involvement in and concern for that very needy situation:

'We have just received two bags of wheat flour, two cartons of protein powder and four cartons of soya bean extract,' I wrote to Jean at that time. 'God is so good to us I could just weep. Just imagine - the severity of the famine is something else and never at any time has any member of this household known what it is like to go to sleep hungry.'

Many other groups and organisations were also trying to help, some by supplying immediate aid and others by encouraging development projects. I became particularly aware of this when a friend brought a tall athletic-looking Irishman to visit me one afternoon. His name was Ken McCormick. A few years previously, a friend had invited him round to his home to watch *Five Minutes to Midnight*, a documentary on world famine. A number of local business people had also been invited. The harsh realities presented on the screen had appalled them all. 'O.K. Maybe we can't do much, but we've got to do *something*,' his friend had said, 'other than simply handing out money.'

The result had been a city-wide partnership with the Kitui region. For the past three years, Ken told me, the people of Waterford had been funding various development projects and seeking to foster contacts at every level with the Akamba people. He and Michael McNena, another committee member, were in Kitui assessing the situation.

I was encouraged by the story. It was heartening to hear how that initial reaction to an emotive documentary had been translated into a meaningful response. Here was a group of people who had not simply given a once-off donation and then allowed the pressures of daily living to wipe those disturbing images from their minds. They wanted to get involved, to give time and thought as well as money - and I could only pray that God would bless their efforts.

1981 got off to a promising start with an excellent rainy season. But though in general things improved, with food becoming plentiful once more, the Baby Home was in a state of crisis. Our water supply, which had always been erratic, had dried up altogether. Every single drop for drinking, washing and cleaning had to be fetched by Land-rover from the river. For an average-size family this would not have been an undue burden, but with a couple of dozen babies all needing, amongst other things, fresh nappies at least six times a day, it was a huge problem.

How well I remember sitting up one night with a wee lassie called Rhoda. Although the famine was over and I had been able to send some children home, others were still being brought to me suffering from severe malnutrition, and Rhoda had been one of the worst Marasmic/ Kwashiorkor cases I had ever seen. After a rocky beginning, her body had begun to respond to food, but that night her fever had suddenly shot up to 106°F. And I had no water - apart from a very little for drinking. It was simply dreadful not having any means of cooling her down.

As the weeks went by and the taps remained dry I was advised to keep the number of children in the Home below twenty. But even with reduced numbers we were taxed to our limits. Night and day, the demand for water seemed to dominate everything else. I was forever borrowing the Bainbridge's Land-rover, lugging drums about, appealing for help to carry them back to the house. And still the place smelt like a sewage works!

'The water situation is dreadful,' I wrote to Jean in March. 'At present we are using salty water from a borehole. I just cannot imagine what the end of all this is going to be.'

Yet again a question-mark was hanging, like a dark cloud, over the future: what would happen when I next went home on leave? The general feeling seemed to be that the Baby Home was no longer viable and would have to close.

'I agree that it is not viable at present, but there is no reason why it should not become viable,' I told Jean. 'And the Church Leaders agree that there is still a very great need of such a work in this area.'

The only answer seemed to be to move the children five miles down the road into Kitui town. From every point of view this would be an advantage. Kitui town was on the bus route, and therefore more accessible than Mulango; it offered much better back-up facilities in the form of shops and the Government Hospital; and most important of all the move would bring us closer to a source of running water.

Accordingly, that April, Reverend Joel Konzi, the Chairman of the Regional Church Council went to see the appropriate government official to inquire whether the government would consider assigning them a free piece of land on which a new Baby Home might be built.

'We are having incredible problems with water here in Mulango so in view of that the Church has applied for a plot in Kitui town upon which to build a proper Baby Home,' I wrote in my July prayer letter. 'I do earnestly covet your prayers for this move. It requires what is to my mind an incredibly large amount of money, but we do believe that we are going ahead in the Lord's will and we are looking forward with excitement to His provision for us.'

Even as I wrote this, a sense of my own audacity all but took my breath away. Father Tommy, a local priest with a wonderful gift for building and design, had estimated that it would cost in the region of £30,000 to build a house suitable for our needs. Of course I had seen God provide before on many occasions - but we had never required anything on that scale!

'In the middle of next month it will be one year since we have had water running in the taps!!' I told Jean in November. 'I *dream* of our new Baby Home in Kitui. I think I will spend one hour per day in the shower giving thanks for water!!'

Eight months had passed since Pastor Konzi had applied for a plot of land and materially-speaking my dream did not seem any closer to realization. Was I building castles in the air, I had asked myself many times during those sticky dusty months of waiting? No - deep down the assurance was there and growing stronger - God would provide.

One particularly humid afternoon Tommy dropped in to say hello. He was a great favourite with the children. Even Kavengi, a little madam who turned up her button nose at the human race in general, adored him. And this afternoon, as on every other occasion, as soon as he appeared in the doorway, she held up her arms. Sweeping her onto his knee, Tommy sat down and wiped his brow.

'What you need in here is cross ventilation,' he informed me.

'Never mind the fancy stuff - a trickle of water coming out of those taps over there would make my day!' I retorted disentangling myself from a couple of pairs of clinging arms to open a bottle of *Sprite*. 'What's cross ventilation anyway?'

He took a pencil from his pocket and began sketching on the back of an envelope, concentrating on the angle of the windows. 'Now if I was building a Baby Home for you, this is what I would do ...'

In ten minutes flat I saw my dream come true. Three buildings arranged in the shape of a 'U': one to house the children, a second to house the girls who helped me with them and the third, constituting the left arm of the 'U' - two bedrooms, an open-plan kitchen and living-room, a toilet and (oh bliss!) a shower - to house me myself personally (as my African friends always said).

'That's fantastic, Tommy!' I gasped. 'That's exactly what I had in mind.'

'Mmm.' Transferring Kavengi onto his left knee, Tommy surveyed his handiwork. 'It *does* look rather impressive on paper. All we need is the money.'

'Money!' I said lightly. 'The money's no problem.'

'Why? Do you have some?'

'No, but I know how to get it.'

'Now Katie,' Tommy looked at me pityingly, 'if you think any organisation is going to dish out £30,000 just like that ...'

'I know,' I interrupted. 'You have to fill up a million

forms in triplicate. My method is much simpler. I pray for it.'

Tommy shoved the envelope back into his pocket. 'Grand,' he said bleakly. 'You pray for it, and in the meantime I'll try and come up with a practical suggestion.'

That was Wednesday. Twenty-four hours later, I presented myself in his office.

'How far would £1000 get us?'

'It would be a good start, if we had it!' replied Tommy. 'Which we don't.'

'Oh yes we do,' I produced the cheque with a flourish and waved it under his nose.

Tommy gaped. 'Where did you get that?'

'Remember those folk from Waterford? Well, their committee just decided to send me a donation. It arrived in the post this morning. All the way from your homeland!'

Poor Tommy! Every other day, for the next six weeks, he had to endure me charging in, wild with excitement, to plant yet another cheque on his desk: £100 one day, £175 the next - then £2,000 (a *small gift*, according to the donor! But what a sacrifice!) on the very day Pastor Konzi informed me that Kitui Town Council had given us a plot of land. Over £5,000 arrived from Holland less than a week later.

And so it went on.

Tommy found a builder and crew and got down to business:

'God has been flooding in all the money we need to build the girls' house and my house, and together with Tommy's amazing abilities these two buildings should be completed before he goes on leave at the beginning of

July - one of them hopefully by the middle of April,' I was able to write in March.

I could not even begin to put into words the overwhelming sense of wonder and gratitude which I was experiencing. Apart from anything else, my financial inundation was the talk of the town. There would have been nothing particularly extraordinary if people had been giving sporadically to the Baby Home over a period of years - it was the number and the suddenness of the gifts that defied rational explanation.

'So how are you going to put a stop to all this money when you don't need any more?' Tommy challenged me, as the walls of the first house rose around us, and still the cheques came rolling in.

'It's out of my hands. But I imagine it'll stop in the same way it started - at exactly the right time, when God sees the job's complete.'

At exactly the right time. How good it was to be so clearly reminded that that is the way God acts. Not a moment too soon - not a moment too late.

At exactly the right time, the first stage of our building project was finished: three bedrooms, a dining-room, living-room, kitchen, two toilets and a shower! I had just long enough to settle eighteen babies and the four girls who helped me to look after them into their new, spotlessly-clean, cross-ventilated premises, before going home on leave.

CHAPTER THIRTEEN

FACING FAMINE AGAIN

Six months later I returned to find my own house practically completed. All it needed was a coat of paint inside and mosquito screening on the windows. More important still, the children were obviously thriving in their new home.

The building work continued in the months which followed. During my furlough many people in Scotland, Ireland, England and Holland had given money which enabled us to start acquiring materials - sand, cement, concrete blocks and crushed stone - for the main block straight away. We needed extra space. Numbers were growing rapidly and soon, in addition to the eighteen children and four girls in the original building, there were twenty-eight children and three girls occupying building number two!

But the money which had been given was not only used to erect buildings. We were also aiming to instal a number of underground water tanks. The water situation in Kitui was better than Mulango (throughout the six months I had been in Scotland, there had been water in the taps - a blessing which continued for several months after my return), but even so, the town supply tended to be erratic, and the Baby Home, situated as it was at the end of a pipe-line, was in a particularly vulnerable position. We needed facilities to collect water during the rainy

season and store it for our personal use - otherwise we
would always be at the mercy of the latest drought, not to
mention the latest burst pipe.

All this building-work, together with the increasing
number of children and the corresponding increase in
staff, added up to a lot more administration than I had
been used to. In Litein we had had a great many children,
but Matthew and Priscilla had been there to share the
load. (Matthew, by the way, had managed Litein Children's Centre so efficiently that the Central Church
Council had recently appointed him as overall supervisor
of the A.I.C. Children's Centres, now seventeen in
number; so I couldn't have asked for a more sympathetic
boss!) In Kitui, as far as the day to day running of the
Home was concerned, the responsibility was all mine,
and when it came to paperwork - ... well, as Tony, the
headmaster of a local school, who brought law and order
to the Baby Home accounts would say, if Kenwood had
ever heard of me they wouldn't have bothered inventing
a mixer. I was so grateful to God both for his help and for
the help of other friends such as Maluki Mwinzi, a teacher
and Mary, his wife. They made the responsibility a much
less lonely business.

Indeed looking back over the years I could see so
many instances of the way God had used caring people to
keep my head above water, and provide for my emotional
needs.

Often during a period of particular stress and difficulty an encouraging letter or tape had arrived, or better
still - some understanding friend or colleague had providentially appeared on the scene. There had been Mrs.
Rookmaaker's timely visit during my early days in
Mulango; the Principal of the Bible School's words of

encouragement when I had been tempted to leave; and later, when the water crisis had been at its worst and the children suffering from all sorts of mysterious illnesses, I had been given a wonderful companion. Joanna was the eighteen year old daughter of a very skilful eye-surgeon. The months that she spent at the Baby Home, between leaving school and beginning her medical studies, were enough to convince me that she, too, would make an excellent doctor. The children loved her and the visitors to the Home loved her, and, just as her father had saved the sight of many many African people, so on many many occasions her bubbling high spirits saved my sanity during those testing months.

By July 1983, following the failure of the April rains, the whole Kitui district was once again plummeted into famine. Amidst widespread misery, the sense of responsibility not only towards our forty-six children, but also towards the local community, weighed more heavily than ever upon me. Imagine the wonderful joy of learning that once again I was to have an additional God-sent support! A letter arrived from Glasgow. It was from Dorothy, one of Jean's daughters. She had just qualified as a nurse and was wondering if I would like her to come and give me a hand for a couple of months. Would I what!! She received her reply post haste and sizzling round the edges with enthusiasm.

Dorothy arrived in January 1984, just as the main block of the Baby Home and our first underground water-tank were nearing completion. How I would ever have coped without her I do not know, for at the end of the month I received some very bad news. A letter arrived from Rona to tell me that Mum had had a cerebral haemorrhage. After the initial shock, I realized that the tone of the letter was reassuring. The general feeling seemed to be that I should not rush home. Mum's condition was stable and the doctor was optimistic that she would make a good recovery. Still, the news left me numbed and shaken, and despite subsequent reassurances, I was uneasy.

I was also hectically busy. Between one thing and another - critically ill children, desperately needy families, problems with staff, queries from builders - there seemed to be an unending stream of demands.

'Katie and I were disturbed most of the night and during the morning. We had a total of twenty-two adults and four children calling at the home!' Dorothy told her folks in a letter shortly after her arrival.

What a blessing it was to have someone to share in the comings and goings! And quite apart from the refreshing effect of her company (as surely as it takes two to make a quarrel, it takes two to fully appreciate the funny side of life!) this partner proved perfectly capable of taking over during those times when I had to be away; when I had to go to Nairobi in search of food, for example, or to Kijabe with a child in need of surgery. It meant so much to know that should a child's condition deteriorate unexpectedly in my absence, Dorothy had both the nursing skill and the initiative to decide on a course of treatment.

At the beginning of June, I was alone again for four weeks while Dorothy travelled to Uganda with an eye-safari team (led by Dr. Mike Absolam, Joanna's father). I missed her very much. At the same time the vague uneasiness which I experienced whenever I rang Scotland to ask how Mum was, became more and more pronounced.

'She's in good form. Don't worry. Just come when

you can,' my sisters kept saying, but the words did little to retard the sense of urgency developing within me. Home had never seemed so far away. I wanted desperately to see Mum. But could I possibly ask Dorothy to run the Baby Home for three months? To postpone the postgraduate course which she was due to start in Scotland, and to cope single-handed with the inevitable food problems, water problems, staff problems and medical problems here in Kitui?

An A.I.M. missionary called Hilary, *had* offered to keep her company, but the situation really required two trained nurses. Should I leave or not? I rang Scotland yet again. 'Well, Mum hasn't really improved over the last wee while, but she's holding her own,' Rona told me. That was it. I telephoned the travel agent and booked my ticket.

Dorothy's reaction to the news that the whole weight of responsibility was about to be landed on her twenty-two-year-old shoulders was quite remarkable.

'I had been praying about Katie's situation,' she wrote to her parents. 'Very gradually I reached the stage where I felt content either to stay and take over or to go home and leave it to someone else. Then I discovered that God and Katie had it all worked out and Katie was leaving in one week! I know the next three months will not be easy but the last month in Uganda was not easy either, and I am sure *now* that God will provide the strength I need.'

Even then I suspected that my decision to return in such a hurry was more than a human impulse.

Mike and Mary Absolam were waiting to meet me at Heathrow airport. Something had happened. I saw bad news written in the sober lines on Mike's normally cheery face.

'Your Mum's just had another cerebral,' he told me gently. 'The message is that you're to travel up to Argyll straight away.'

I caught the night-sleeper to Glasgow with one minute to spare. Alison, Dorothy's sister (George and Jean were away at the time) was waiting at the station in Glasgow and told me to take her mother's car for the rest of the journey. Three hours later I joined my family at the hospital to find Mum unconscious but still alive.

After a few hours rest I returned to her bedside. 'How are you, Mum?' I sat down and took her work-roughened hand in mine. At the sound of my voice, she stirred slightly; then opened her eyes, and, in a moment filled with loving recognition, welcomed me with a smile.

Less than a week later, a few days after her eighty-third birthday, she died, without ever fully regaining consciousness. Together with Dad, Jessie, Rona, their husbands and families, I grieved my loss. Mum had held a very special place in all our hearts. Her death was the first major break in the family-circle and we felt it deeply.

Meanwhile, as famine continued to rage in Kitui, Dorothy somehow found time not only to look after fifty-two children, but to write detailed letters home. It certainly eased my mind to hear how well she was coping despite worsening conditions, and as I read I could only praise God for the evident faith, wisdom and sense of humour (arguably the key to survival!) those letters displayed. Since they also constituted a unique record of daily life at the Baby Home, with her permission, I would like to share a few extracts from them.

9th July

Malusi came to see me and in a nice way was checking that I realized the importance of daily morning worship with the girls.

10th July

Kimansi (the gardener) came to tell me that there seemed to be a leak in our mains water pipe. (Water is more precious than gold!) I drove down to the polytechnic to get the plumber, then went to look for milk again. Still no U.H.T. milk and no more maize meal.

As we were preparing the children for supper, Kimansi came to tell me that the children's toilet was blocked. The plumber was not overjoyed to see me again!

14th July

Pastor Konzi wanted to see me this afternoon. It turned out to be a summit meeting comprising Konzi, Malusi, Mr. Kangethe (Child Welfare Officer) and me!

There's a problem family - a mentally defective couple and their four very badly nourished children. The church was prepared to supply the food, and Malusi would distribute it but did we really think that the younger children would be adequately cared for by the parents? I agreed to go to the hospital to see the two younger children (one is three years and the other four years old but they look about one year and two years old). They are not too bright mentally and are certainly starved though not critically ill at the moment.

In the end I decided it would be much better for the children and less worrying for all of us if I admitted these two as my share in the burden.

Katie did not want me to take more because I already have fifty-two children, but this seemed a better answer at the time.

18th July

People are coming every day needing help with food. Absolutely *nothing* is growing - and what the girls call *shortings* (i.e. shortages) are becoming a problem.

1st August

This evening I had to draw the girls' attention to the fact that water flowing out under the sink in the Baby Home needs to be reported! Another job for the plumber. But when he left water started flowing from the pipe leading *to* the taps.

Do you think he really is a plumber??

30th August

On Wednesday I went to the Government Office and stood in a queue to get a permit to buy maize. I only bought a few sacks because they were underweight yet they were being sold at the full price.

I have to give antibiotic by injection to a little fellow called Mark. He has a dreadful ear infection. He has almost no muscle tone and I feel shattered when I have to inject him. Yesterday a little boy who is in the same room as Mark said to me in Kikamba: 'You shouldn't keep coming to make that one cry.'

At which point I could have cried myself!

4th September

An eleven year old girl arrived with her father. She is called Ngina. She has absolutely no hair, a completely vacant face, a very wasted upper body and arms, and gross oedema and skin loss of her legs. Her legs also have sores (and flies!) all over them. She has so much fluid retention that the soles of her feet are curved out so that she can't stand.

What a tragic picture!

6th September

We are getting on amazingly well here, in spite of the desperate famine. The fact that there are no serious problems of relationships is surely an answer to prayer. I am exceedingly grateful.

We have a few surprises for Katie coming back. Some big ones and some small ones. The best is forty-two thousand gallons of water. We had a lot of rain for three nights.

But I have just had to admit twins because their mother seems to be totally neglecting them and they could easily die.

The famine is awful. The families of the children who are now getting better are all struggling to stay alive. There is no prospect of sending them home.

In October I returned to Kitui, and Dorothy returned to Scotland to begin a post-graduate course in sick children's nursing. She had done a mammoth amount of work in my absence. Her letters had not told the half of it. Waiting for me at the Baby Home I found over sixty smiling children, a contented staff, impeccable records and a newly decorated house! My heart was still very sore after Mum's death, but Dorothy's practical and loving preparations for my home-coming combined with Tony's faithful book-work meant that I was able to pick up the reins of responsibility as if I'd never been away, simply carrying on where she had left off.

The famine worked up to its zenith. With cots in every available space, we managed to squeeze around eighty children into the Home, while feeding about seven hundred people outside on a weekly basis. Our official supplies from the relief agencies were by no means geared to cater for such numbers, but by this stage I had almost ceased to be surprised when someone with a sackful of milk powder appeared at the gate on the very day when the last of our own had been used up. Just as, in the early days, God had faithfully provided food for my household of five, so now He provided for our household of almost one hundred. There were times when from one meal to the next we did not know *how* we were going to eat, but eat we did; like the widow of Zarapeth, my jar of oil and supply of flour never ran out. And finally in December a huge consignment of clothes, food, medicine and equipment arrived from Scotland. All had been supplied by the loving friends who had heard of our need and had been transported to our very doorstep free of charge. These gifts carried us right through to the time when food at a reasonable price became available in the shops once more.

At long last the famine was over! Throughout Kitui the people held services of thanksgiving, first for the rains and then for the harvest. Their days of exuberant rejoicing, though, were tragically cut short. That February a cholera outbreak of epidemic proportions swept through the district, proving the fatal blow to hundreds of bodies already weakened by lack of proper nourishment. Families were decimated. A quarter of a mile from the Baby Home, in the cream-painted A.I.C. church building with its simple cross over the doorway, Pastor Konzi presided over one funeral after another. Why? I could not help asking. Why should people who have endured so much already have to suffer in this way?

The cholera epidemic was followed by a particularly virulent outbreak of measles. More deaths; and this time the Baby Home was affected as badly as anywhere else.

'There are twenty-one children with measles today and four more cooking,' I wrote to Jean at the beginning of March. 'I've turned the front hall into an extra isolation room. It's a blessing we sent thirty-four home, otherwise they would also be sick by now.'

Over three weeks went by before I was able to finish that letter. During that period, I literally lived through a nightmare. The sick children required round the clock nursing-care, and though the girls did their best to help, the vast majority could not be left unsupervised. Hour after hour, night after night, I gave fluids, ice-baths, injections - everything I could think of in an attempt to win the battle for those twenty-five lives. But despite all our efforts and all our prayers six children died; two darling, chubby, hitherto healthy wee girls within hours of each other.

When I came home that day, after my second trip to the mortuary, I lay on my bed and sobbed my heart out. I just couldn't stop crying - not even when one of the girls looked in to say that Pastor Konzi was waiting to speak to me. A few minutes later Pastor Konzi himself appeared in the doorway. He was an old man - a father to the church, with a true pastor's heart, full of patience, wisdom and love. And now he sat down on the chair by my bed.

'Tell me why you are crying?' he asked.

'It's so terribly hard to understand...' I sobbed. 'The mortuary is packed with bodies from ceiling to floor... one on top of the other...'

He understood. He knew I wasn't asking him to quote Scripture verses or make theological statements. At that point, I simply couldn't have coped with them.

'We, ourselves are used to this kind of thing, Katie,' he said quietly.

His faith was so much stronger than mine.

'I don't know where God is in it all. I don't even have time to talk to Him any more,' I gulped.

Again he soothed me. 'You are too tired to read and pray. I will come every day and I will pray with you and God will give us strength and carry us through...'

From then on, throughout those traumatic weeks, Pastor Konzi came every single day, sometimes bringing two or three other Pastors with him. They read the Bible to us and encouraged us, no matter how hard it seemed, to keep hoping and trusting...

'We poured our hearts out in prayer for the babies and six still died, but the other nineteen, who were equally sick, lived,' I told Jean, when I eventually got round to finishing my letter.

'At the end of it all I am hanging on to the knowledge that my Redeemer liveth, that He, the Judge of all the earth always does right, even when I do not understand it at all!'

CHAPTER FOURTEEN

HIS LOVE BREAKS THROUGH

'I'm so tired, I just pray I'm not going nuts or something!'

It was the first letter I'd written to Jean for almost two months. The famine was over. The children were well. Everything and everyone seemed to have bounced back to life - apart from me. Somehow I just couldn't shake off the build-up of exhaustion. 'I seem to spend my time screeching at the girls,' I scrawled, before laying down my pen, with a guilty sigh.

My penitence, even then, was tempered with exasperation. I loved the girls, but sometimes they seemed to take more out of me than their charges. They came to the Baby Home, chosen by Church Leaders, from families in difficult circumstances, to help look after the children. After spending some time with us, many of them would have their fees paid by people in Scotland to go for a course of further training, which would, hopefully, enable them to escape from the poverty trap.

In principle the idea was a good one. The main problem, from my point of view, was that they had never been taught to think for themselves. At home they had deferred to their fathers and brothers. One day they would defer to their husbands. In the meantime, they needed constant supervision, gazing at me, eyes large with uncomprehending compliance, as I scolded over the latest failure to report a sick child, or a leaking pipe, or the fact that we were almost out of washing powder.

There were, however, exceptions: some of the girls had real initiative and leadership ability. Masaa, for example, a deeply committed Christian girl, had shown herself quite capable of anticipating and averting those minor domestic crises which were forever driving me scatty. As time had gone on I had realized that she could communicate with the staff far more effectively than I. Now she was about to begin her nurse's training. When she had finished, we both hoped that she would take over the Baby Home from me. The prospect filled me with a deep satisfaction. Masaa was so right for the job. The question was whether I would be able to stick the pace until then? Wearily, I took up my pen once more:

'Some people were asking me could the church not start a similar ministry up in M--. For sure a Baby Home is badly needed up there, but I'm not even going to think about it until this one is in the African hands of God's choosing. As far as I am aware that is Masaa, which means about a five year wait - by which time, Jean, I would be fifty-two years old *if* I live that long!! (Take time out to weep at this stage!).'

The door opened. A small figure slipped in like a shadow, spotted me at the table and literally leapt into my arms.

'John, you rascal! Just what do you think you're up to?' Casting the letter aside, I buried my face for a moment in the little boy's curly head, remembering... John had almost died during the measles outbreak and had suffered from anorexia for weeks afterwards. I'd had to be so strict with him; threatening, cajoling, spanking and bribing to make him eat. I had absolutely *hated* doing it. But he was well now, and instinctively seemed to have

grasped the fact that I had acted out of love - for here he
was sneaking in for a cuddle.

'How utterly stupid of me to imagine for one minute
that I couldn't keep going with kids like you around,' I
murmured, hugging him close. 'All your Mama needs is
a bit of a rest, isn't that right, dote?'

'Why not stay here with Fred and me for a couple of
days?' Jan suggested on my next trip to Nairobi. It
seemed like an excellent idea at the time. I had come to
Nairobi to buy nappies only to discover it was a public
holiday and the shops were shut. By taking up my
friend's kind invitation I could kill two birds with one
stone; save a wasted journey *and* have an opportunity to
put my feet up.

Accordingly I relaxed on Monday, bought my nappies on Tuesday morning and roared back into the
grounds of the Baby Home early on Tuesday evening.

'Is everything O.K.? You didn't have any problems
while I was away?' I asked one of the girls, as she helped
me carry my parcels into the house.'

'Oh no, Katie. It was fine,' she smiled.

'That's good,' I said, totally unreassured. Things
were always 'fine' if one were to judge by first reports.
The word meant little more than that, as I could see for
myself, the house was still standing. I knew I would have
to ask specific questions to uncover the significant details.

'Does that mean all the children are well then?'

'Yes, they are all well ...' the girl hesitated briefly and
I braced myself for the bad news ... 'but Sulupi is sick.'

Sulupi was not a child. She was one of the girls, and

had actually been with me for longer than most. When all was said and done I had a particularly soft spot for her. It was not just because she had experience and could work very well when she chose, it was because of her personality... her warmth, her openness. She had a smile like sunlight.

There was not the faintest glimmer of sunlight on her face when I went in to see her that afternoon. She was lying limp on her bed and scarcely seemed able to open her eyes. She had malaria, she told me.

I dosed her with malaria medicine and a glass of hot milk, but was not at all convinced that we had got to the bottom of the trouble.

'Keep an eye on her and let me know *at once* if she gets any worse,' I instructed her room-mates before going to bed that night.

Sulupi did not get any worse over the next forty-eight hours, nor did she get any better; and then on Thursday, she suddenly developed an agonising pain in her abdomen. I prescribed two panadol and fussed around like a clucking hen. 'If she still has the pain by this evening, I'm going to take her to the hospital,' I told the girls.

At four o'clock that afternoon one of them took me aside. I did not need to worry about Sulupi any more, she confided. My momentary relief was transformed into a numbing horror as she proceeded to tell me why: Sulupi, apparently, had had a criminal abortion performed while I had been away. There was now no need for me to take her to the hospital, the girl explained. That morning the baby had come out. One of the other girls had taken it, wrapped it in a cloth and thrown it down the pit latrine.

As she said those words, it was as if the bottom dropped out of my world. Here, in this very Home - a place of refuge dedicated to the Lord and to the little ones He loved so dearly - a baby had been murdered. I turned on my heel, went into my room, sat down, and stared blankly at the bedroom wall. How long I sat there, I do not know. Hour after hour I struggled to come to terms with the spiritual implications of what I had just heard ... the terrible sin against God...

The following morning I tried to contact Pastor Konzi. He was out of town and it was late afternoon before, with the help of a friend, I eventually located him. As soon as he heard my story, he came straight to the home and questioned the girls. As I had suspected Sulupi had not devised the scheme all by herself. Another girl had brought her to the abortionist and later dispensed with the child.

Pastor Konzi looked old, tired and very worn when he came to the end of his discussion with the girls.

'We must send for the police, Katie,' he said.

'Must we? ... Oh yes, I suppose we must!'

Until that moment the legal aspect of what had happened had not even struck me. But now I realized that induced abortion was totally against the law in Kenya, so naturally the police would have to be informed.

Within the hour a blue-shirted officer was escorting Sulupi, her friend, and a third girl (who claimed to have seen Sulupi's friend putting the baby's body into the toilet) off to the cells. 'You ought to have come to us about this immediately!'

He was clearly not at all impressed with my handling of the affair.

At 1:15 a.m. the telephone rang, and I was told that I could pick up two of the girls from the station. Sulupi, though, would have to stay. My heart ached for her. She was still sick and my every instinct told me to go down to the police station and plead to be allowed to bring her home at least for the rest of the night. But I knew it would be pointless.

By Monday Sulupi had revealed the identity of the abortionist and was now in hospital. She would stand trial as soon as she was well enough. 'But we cannot understand why you did not report the matter to us immediately,' the police officer who had come to the Home reiterated before leaving. Because of the delay he and his men had failed to retrieve the body. They had found the cloth the child had been wrapped in, but that was all.

It soon became clear that I too would have to appear in court - to give evidence initially, but there was some concern that I might be implicated in the affair. Sulupi's friend had been heard to boast that she and the abortionist were planning to bribe their way to freedom. She had made a statement to the effect that *I* had aborted Sulupi's baby.

'Sulupi is still in prison but is to be allowed probation pending a favourable report by the Probation Department on the 21st of this month.' I wrote to Jean. 'They have been to see me about it and I have tried to be faithful in showing them Sulupi as I see her. I cannot think that a term in prison (and her crime calls for seven years in prison here) would help either Sulupi or the community. She would be consorting with hardened criminals and the outcome would be nightmarish to consider. The abortionist is to have his trial on 4th September and I have to go and give evidence at it.'

In my anxiety for Sulupi and the daily battle with physical exhaustion, I did not have any energy left to worry about my own position. Theoretically I knew that it might turn nasty; that the abortionist might succeed in making a deal; that the magistrate might well be biased against me because I was white; that if the worst came to the worst I might face a fourteen year prison sentence. But it was the significance of the locked door on the wooden latrine that haunted my waking thoughts. As far as the trial was concerned I simply longed to get it over with...

Finally the day came.

I stood before the magistrate and recounted my side of the story.

Some minutes later, still in a semi-daze, I heard Sulupi's friend testify that *I* had aborted Sulupi.

The magistrate tapped his pencil on the desk: 'Are you telling me that someone who left her own home, her own country and her own people and has lived here all this time looking after our children - that suddenly one day she would get up and decide to kill a baby?'

'I am only saying what the lawyer told me to say,' she muttered.

Sulupi received a two year prison sentence, which, to my great relief, was later commuted to a period on probation.

With the trial over, at long last I was free to go home on furlough. Masaa had volunteered to look after the Baby Home while I was away.

'Hopefully a prayer letter will be sent out telling a wee bit more about my stay at home, but I am probably not going to do any deputation work until the spring. I am more tired this time than I have ever been,' I told my prayer-partners.

I did not wish to burden them with unedifying details; to admit that I felt, spiritually and physically, like a burned out shell - that I could neither see properly, nor hear properly, nor stand in the one place for more than a couple of minutes for fear of fainting.

'Once I get back to Scotland and have a bit of a rest, I will be fine,' I tried to reassure myself.

But it did not quite work out that way. No sooner was I back in Bonnie Scotland, and relaxing in the warmth of Jean and George's home, than I was laid flat on my back with an attack of malaria which lasted for the best part of a fortnight, and left me feeling more wiped out than ever.

That Christmas, I hit an all time low. At one level I was almost convinced that I would never be normal again and I felt terribly guilty about being such a lethargic lump of misery at a time when everyone else was doing their best to be cheerful and festive. Never had it seemed to take so much effort to accomplish next to nothing! Yet although physically and emotionally there seemed to be very little improvement in my state of health from one week to the next, on the spiritual level something very significant was going on. In the midst of my weakness, God's presence was more real to me than it had been for months. It was as if I had emerged from some dark spiritual tunnel to find Him waiting in the stillness, confronting me with a question - one of the most searching questions I had ever been asked in my life: 'What sort of a God do you think I am?'

I found myself looking back over my experiences of the past fourteen years:

'You are a God who guides,' I said.

'You are a God who acts on behalf of the helpless.'

'You are a God who provides for my material needs.'

'You are a God who makes impossibilities possible.'

Yet somehow all these answers seemed to miss the mark, leaving the question more insistent than ever.

'What sort of a God do you think I am?'

I thought back over the events of the past twelve months: 'You are a God of judgement. You hate sin. You condemn. You punish.'

The thought was a revelation to me. Of course at the time of my conversion I had encountered a God of love and forgiveness, but somehow over the years that encounter had never quite overthrown the harsh concept of my childhood. In my heart of hearts, I realized, I still saw God not primarily as a loving Father, but as a Judge. That was why at times I had found it so difficult to rely on Him for comfort and encouragement, despite the many proofs I had been given of His tender care for me and for the children.

The realization was the start of a process of spiritual reappraisal. What, I had to ask myself, was the biblical picture of God? In my questioning I was reminded of the conflict in my own heart with regard to Sulupi. I loved her, yet could never condone the thing which she had done. I had hated the very thought of her going to prison, yet had had to allow the process of justice to take its course. It struck me that in a very small way this conflict between love and justice in my own experience could reflect something of God's attitude to fallen humanity. I had not really thought of it that way before.

Little by little a more biblical picture of God began to filter from my head to my heart. Things finally fell into place at the end of May, when I attended a series of seminars conducted by Selwyn Hughes. In the course of one of his lectures he challenged us to examine the source of our security and self-worth. Was it in our work? In a marriage relationship? In the lives of our children? Or was it in God Himself? For the rooting of our security, our self-worth and our significance in Him was, he maintained, the key both to psychological health and spiritual fulfilment.

Six months previously I might have assented to this in theory, but inwardly I would have balked at the idea. My main source of identity and security had always been in my work and in close relationships; and I could not have brought myself to abandon myself totally to God, because basically I was still afraid of Him. But now my picture of God had undergone a subtle transformation. As Selwyn Hughes spoke, I realized that I was being invited to leave behind the feelings of failure which had plagued me during my low periods and to ground myself joyfully and unquestioningly in the love of God. Contradictory though it may sound, having recognized that there was no clenched fist about to hammer me if I refused the invitation, I discovered I could say 'Yes, You are enough Lord. I don't need anything or anyone else apart from You,' and really mean it.

In the weeks which followed there was no dramatic transformation in either my character or my health (the latter was improving, although progress was much slower than I would have liked); but it ceased to matter that I still did not know when I would be fit to return to Kenya. I had taken an important step forward and was learning, at long last, not to evaluate myself according to what I did, but according to who I was in Christ. I no longer saw myself primarily as Katie, a wiped-out missionary on furlough - but as Katie, the child of the King of Love.

'I've booked your ticket,' said Elisabeth. 'You're flying from London with Kenya Airways on 24th November.'

'I don't know where I would be without you,' I beamed.

It was mid-October and I was in the A.I.M. office in London. At long last the doctor had given me a clean bill of health.

'But remember! It's disciplined off-duty times from now on,' Alan reminded me with mock-severity.

I beamed again. I was really very grateful to the staff at the London Office, appreciating more than ever the wonderful family relationship within the Mission. It is always there, but becomes particularly evident when a member of the family is ill, or in real trouble of one kind or another. Throughout the months of uncertainty I had received a great deal of loving support, and they were now as pleased as I was that everything had finally fallen into place.

'I'll be out in the new year to make sure you're behaving yourself,' was Alan's parting shot.

The New Year. What would it bring? I wondered, as muffled to my eyebrows against the cold, I made my way to Euston station. The letters which I carried in my handbag gave some clues. There was the one from Matthew telling me that Sulupi would be staying with himself and Priscilla for the next few months. There was the one from Masaa with the good news that all the children were well, and that she had been accepted into the nursing school in Kijabe. And there were several from prayer partners, all enclosing money towards the building of a special unit for handicapped children.

'It is such a privilege, such a very great privilege to see the way You work things out, Lord ...' I thought as I climbed into my bunk in the night-sleeper. '... the way You are providing for the children, the handicapped ones especially. I know how precious they are in Your sight.'

'Yes, they are precious to Me, but so are You,' came the unexpected reminder.

Ah, that was one very special lesson I would be taking back with me to Kenya.

Doors slammed. With a sigh of thankfulness I relaxed against my pillows. They are precious ... I am precious... all are precious ...

Effortlessly the train slid from the station and surged out into the night...

AFTERWORD
by
Lynda Neilands

Katie has ended her story (for the time being) in the autumn of 1986. Three months before that, while it was still uncertain when she would be fit to return to Kenya, she made a brief trip to Ireland to speak to various groups about her work. My husband and I were asked to give her hospitality whilst she was in Waterford. 'You should have a lot in common,' Ken, the organiser, assured us. He never spoke a truer word.

From the moment Katie stepped across the threshold of our home, we knew we were going to be friends. There was an instant bond. A strong similarity of approach and understanding. We shared the same spiritual values. The same things reduced us to tears of helpless laughter (and laughter is never in short supply when Katie is around!). It was as if we had known each other all our lives. 'You'll have to come and visit me when I get back to Kenya,' she said to me after a mere six hours acquaintance.

That night I hardly slept a wink. The suggestion had thrown me into a state of panic. Much as I like and identified with Katie, visiting a Baby Home was the last thing I felt inclined to do. The sort of visitor our new friend needed would be practical, with medical training or building ability, or at least the knack of changing nappies. All I had to recommend myself was an all-tovivid imagination. Yet somehow I couldn't dismiss the invitation from my mind.

And the following afternoon I discovered why. 'Oh, you write, do you?' Katie remarked as I plonked my typewriter down on the dining-room table. (Writing had recently become something more than a hobby where I was concerned.) 'My mission keep telling me I should write a book about my experiences but I haven't the first clue how to go about it.'

A car-horn sounded and she breezed off to her next speaking engagement. But her parting words seemed to hang on the air with a spiritual resonance which was promptly interpreted by my husband. He had overheard the exchange and now stepped out of the study. 'You know what. I think you should offer to help with that book,' he said.

Katie, we were to discover, thought so too. Praying about the possibility of recording her experiences, then arriving into the home of two total strangers to discover that one of them was a writer was, in her view, more than a coincidence.

My own reaction was one of excitement mixed with caution. It was one thing discussing a book over coffee. It was another gathering sufficient information to write it. And quite another finding a publisher willing to commit the manuscript to print.

Yet step by step all these obstacles were overcome. Holidays took me to Scotland. Work took me to London. Both sets of circumstances enabled me to spend more time with Katie, to meet some of her closest friends and associates, to (psychologically) pressurize her into staying in the one room long enough to record her story to tape.

Most encouraging of all was my coincidental meeting with a Christian publisher who expressed a strong interest in seeing an outline and a couple of specimen chapters of the book.

None of this surprised Katie. 'That's the sort of thing that God does when the children are concerned,' she smiled. 'He's making it possible for more people to become aware of His fatherly love for the smallest and the least in human terms.'

The possibility became a reality. Katie returned to Kenya in the Autumn of 1986. I visited her there the following January. And the Autumn of 1988 saw the publication of *Love Breaks Through*. Within a week of publication the first print-run had sold out!

'Out of suffering comes blessing.' Those are the words which spring to mind as I look back over God's dealings. The evident appeal of this book would seem one more precious fruit emerging from the very testing period of her life which Katie shares in its final chapters.

And God has seen fit to give her life-story an on-going ministry. Today, as children continue to suffer and die in appalling numbers over our globe, many of us are all too painfully aware of our own limitations and failings. I rejoice that the message of *Love Breaks Through* is there for encouragement. God cares for the children. And he is supernaturally able to do in and through us, the things we cannot do for ourselves.

Love Breaks Through
retold for younger readers.

A FRIEND FOR LIFE
Lynda Neilands

Katie loves babies. At home on the farm there were baby
lambs, baby kittens and puppies and even baby rabbits!

In the big hospital where she worked there was a
special place for baby boys and girls.

In Kenya she looked after babies whose parents could
not take care of them.

Life is never quiet or easy when there's twenty or
thirty babies in your house, but Katie sees God working
in her life and in the lives of people around her.

pocket paperback

ISBN 1 871676 78 9   128 pages

More
inspiring life stories
from
Christian Focus Publications

CHANGING STEP
Jill Beatty

"What an exciting life . . . So frank and honest, that it is real and living. This book ministers to those who need strength, to those who need a comforter, to those who proclaim a living Saviour".

From the foreword by Colin Peckham, Principal, Faith Mission Bible College.

Following her teenage years in London during World War Two, Jill Beatty joined the army. She was in Palestine when the modern state of Israel was created. There she enjoyed life to the full. Her pursuit of happiness was relentless and yet did not meet with success during her time there. Enter Rex, a handsome army major who was eventually to become her husband.

Everything changed and eventually Jill herself was changed.

Trouble and difficulty became a regular part of her life. Difficulties during her husband's death and in her family. Through them all, her new faith upheld her and she is a shining example of how God provides for those who trust in Him and ensures that they have the victory.

pocket paperback

ISBN 1 871676 68 1   160 pages

A HUNDRED HOUSES
Anne Rayment

Life as a missionary is often seen as romantic, but Irene Rowley tells of the reality - coping with disease, misunderstanding, a handicapped child and homesickness. Yet her determination to work for God in Brazil carries her through and gives purpose to all that she does.

David Waite writes: "People will be challenged after reading this down-to-earth, honest book. We learn of the tensions of missionary life, the heat, dust and squalor of Brazil and of some of the problems of the people there. It is refreshingly different."

Irene Rowley and her husband, Joe, have worked in Brazil with Unevangelised Fields Mission since 1966.

pocket paperback

ISBN: 1 871676 77 0   160 pages

MUSSELS AT MIDNIGHT
Stephen Anderson

"Stephen Anderson is the freshest breath of fresh air to blow through the Church of Scotland for a long time ... I have been fascinated and deeply challenged by my brother's life story ..." William Still, Aberdeen

"... from a farm in Perthshire to the Ministry of the Gospel ..."

On the ski slopes or in the Church, in the company of people of all ages Stephen Anderson communicates the Gospel.

The power of this Gospel changed his life. This book tells us how this happened and how his work is to share this life changing power with all he meets.

Told in his own words in a frank and humble way.

pocket paperback

ISBN: 0 0906731 93 3   160 pages

THE ONLY WAY TO WALK
Sheana Brown

Personal courage and amazing faith in God's loving care are the hallmarks of James Brown's testimony. A terrible accident at his factory robbed him of both legs and very nearly cost him his life.

Yet this remarkable man recovered and has led an active life with the assistance of his family and friends.

His appetite for travel, his enthusiastic evangelistic work and his contacts with deep-sea fishermen from many different countries all testify to James Brown's determination to overcome his disability and lead a normal life.

This story contains many incidents which shows the support James has had from the Christian community. More importantly, they show God at work in his life.

pocket paperback

ISBN: 1 871676 43 6   160 pages

OUT OF THE TIGER'S MOUTH
Dr Charles H Chao

Born in China in 1916, Charles Chao is, in the words of Dr Loraine Boettner, "a man of God - with untiring devotion".

His life's work has been for China. Despite persecution from Chinese communists, narrow escapes from prison and death, Charles Chao has not ceased to translate major Christian works for his fellow countrymen.

This book tells the exciting story of this man's life -

how God continually provided for the specific needs of his family, his work and himself. As you read this book, you will be amazed with God's timing and how God's plan is being unfolded for China.

J G Vos, who for a time was principal of Yingkou Bible Seminary and Samuel E Boyle, South China missionary, both feature in a significant way in Mr Chao's life. Dr Chao's family are all Christians and some of them are actively involved in mission work to the Chinese. Dr Chao and his wife now live in the USA, from where they have travelled widely, reminding the Christian world of their responsibility to the great Chinese nation.

pocket paperback

ISBN: 1 871676 59 2 160 pages

DYING TO LIVE
William Still

William Still's life has always been linked with Aberdeen. Born, brought up and educated in 'the granite city' he has also devoted 45 years to the city centre pastorate of Gilcomston South Church. His ministry has reached out across the nation and the world inspired by a single-minded commitment to the gospel.

He is a spokesman and example for those who believe that a faithful and firm stance on the essentials of the faith results in lifestyle changes in individuals and communities. As you read his own words, you will be challenged by the many individuals who have been influenced by his ministry and witness to the truth of Scripture.

Now over eighty years old he is 'Still - Dying to Live'
and a shining example of the kind of pastor our society
needs.

B format

ISBN: 0 906731 97 6   192 pages